A GUIDE TO GET

Teaching

Written by Jeff Riley
Edited by Suzanne Straw

TROTMAN

In association with UCAS

Jeffrey Riley is a Careers Adviser at the University of North London. **Suzanne Straw** is Senior Consultant at EUCLID – a consultancy in education and training.

This first edition published in 1997
by Trotman and Company Ltd
– in association with UCAS –
12 Hill Rise, Richmond, Surrey TW10 6UA

© Trotman and Company Limited 1997

British Library Cataloguing in Publication Data
A catalogue record for this book is available from the
British Library.

ISBN 0 85660 311 2

Printed and bound in Great Britain

CONTENTS

Chapter One
INTRODUCTION

Teaching as a career is so different from any other that it is particularly important that, if you are considering it, you establish whether it is the right move for you. This book is designed to help readers make that decision and to help explain the increasingly varied training routes and institutions available for potential teachers. The book mainly concentrates on primary and secondary education but also takes a look at teaching in Further and Higher Education and at teaching English as a foreign language.

Education is so rarely out of the headlines that the vital role teachers play in society seems beyond question. Few other jobs offer the chance to make a lasting difference to people's lives. And all the hyped promises of classroom technology, all the hardware and software, will disappoint without that vital piece of peopleware – the teacher. A recent survey of the general public found that the value of teachers to society was rated above that of lawyers, industrialists and even those in the emergency services: teachers came second only to doctors.

☐ WHY CONSIDER TEACHING AS A CAREER?

Teaching is popular as a career choice. Amongst a recent sample of 1000 university finalists it was of greater interest than public relations, computing and even advertising and only slightly behind broadcasting. The five most important reasons cited in the survey for considering teaching as a career were:

*   intellectual challenge
*   long-term career opportunities
*   opportunity to be creative and original
*   opportunity to work with people
*   opportunity for foreign travel.

1

Other significant factors were 'responsibility', 'high starting salary' and 'long-term job security'.

☐ IS THERE A DEMAND FOR TEACHERS?

There is certainly a demand for teachers. There are 440,000 teachers in primary and secondary education in England and Wales. Simply maintaining this number requires 23,000 recruits each year and this already high demand is set to increase. By 2001, an extra 10,000 teachers will need to be trained to cover increases in pupil numbers and a larger than usual number of teachers reaching retirement age over the next five years. These estimates are not based on educated guesses. Teaching is one of the few professions to benefit from sophisticated manpower planning based on factors such as retirement rates and numbers of pupils. This process tells us that, by 2001, there will need to be a 50 per cent increase in the number of recruits for secondary training and recruitment numbers for primary training will have to increase by one-third. In some subjects, the demand will be even more dramatic. Mathematics, for example, will require a 75 per cent increase in the number of recruits.

☐ TEACHING AS A VOCATION

Teaching may attract those drawn to long-term job security or a good starting salary but above all it seeks those who feel teaching is their *vocation*. Frankly, this level of commitment is necessary to cope with the demands the job undoubtedly involves. Teaching is not an 8.45 am to 3.30 pm job. Even the longer holidays are partly taken up with preparing lessons, writing reports and keeping up-to-date with subjects. Part of the pressure comes from the fact that the profession seems easy to criticise. Teachers have to listen to criticism from teaching inspectors, parents, journalists, politicians and, not least, from pupils. One of the reasons that recruitment is an urgent priority is that, in the face of increased pressures, many older teachers have chosen early retirement. Indeed, many students on Post Graduate Certificate in Education (PGCE) courses decide there must be easier ways of earning a living and 25 per cent of them do not, in the end, go into teaching. In 1996, there was a marked fall in the number of applicants, especially mature applicants, for teacher training courses. In primary teaching, there is a continuing shortage of male applicants who may be deterred by what is perceived as its relatively low pay in the long term. A further pick-up in the labour market may well accentuate this pattern.

On a positive note, the profession is coming towards the end of a period of disruptive changes which has seen a new Education Bill virtually every year for the last 14 years. The National Curriculum has become a part of the fabric of teaching and the Standard Assessment Tests are becoming a less difficult issue in schools. For those who do make a commitment to teaching, it can offer a deeply rewarding career which, though demanding physically, emotionally and intellectually, gives back a lot. New entrants to the profession speak enthusiastically of the variety and engaging nature of the career.

This chapter looks at the ways in which state schools can be managed and at the following sectors of the England and Wales education system:

- primary education
- secondary education
- further education
- special needs provision
- the independent sector.

It also looks at Scotland's and Northern Ireland's education systems.

☐ PRIMARY EDUCATION

What is primary education?
In England and Wales the structure of provision can vary markedly in different areas. There are four different levels:

5-7 years	lower primary
5-11/12 years	primary
7-11/12 years	upper primary
7/9-14 years	middle

These may be separate schools entirely or combined as a single school. Schools can also vary in terms of their size, location and the nature of their catchment area with smaller schools having as few as two teachers and larger schools having up to 30 staff and a pupil population of 400. The vast majority of primary schools teach both boys and girls.

What do primary teachers do?
Primary teachers are responsible for teaching the whole range of subjects in the National Curriculum together with religious education. They take their own class for all subjects in contrast to the subject-based specialist teaching found in secondary schools, and

in some middle schools. The National Curriculum gives the framework for primary education and the national system for assessment and evaluation at seven and eleven and the 'baseline assessments' announced in October 1996 for all pupils entering primary education. However, teachers are expected to be able to recognise and monitor the specific individual needs of their pupils and devise imaginative classes and activities that help them fulfil their potential. A primary teacher, for example, might organise a trip to a local food market, set up a market in class, help children prepare some different types of food and, in a multi-national class, might even involve grandparents talking about their national dishes. Such activities would cover many of the following key areas that primary teachers are expected to develop:

- the ability to use spoken and written English language (and the Welsh language in Wales)
- the ability to deal with numbers and explore mathematical ideas
- a knowledge of science and technology through designing, making and problem-solving
- a knowledge of the world we live in, our country, its history and of other countries and their people
- an aesthetic awareness through work in the creative and performing arts.

Teachers are also expected to help the school make links with the local community and to get to know pupils' families as well as professionals in other fields. Junior schools are increasingly employing additional subject specialists to take the lead in developing the area of their subject on behalf of the whole school. In some of the larger primary schools, class teachers take joint responsibility for the year group and work together to plan classes and share the teaching.

How do you train to work in primary schools?
Most teachers train to teach the whole age range but some courses may offer a chance to specialise in 'lower' or 'upper' primary. The most popular route into primary teaching is through a teaching degree, either a BEd or a three or four year BA or BSc course which also awards Qualified Teacher Status (QTS). However, it is also possible to train via a degree and then via a Post Graduate Certificate in Education (PGCE) in primary teaching.

What's included in primary teacher training courses?
Teacher training courses include a significant amount of teaching
practice (32 weeks on four-year BEd courses, 24 weeks on three year
course, 18 weeks on the PGCE and 40 weeks on the School Centred
Inital Teacher Training schemes). Primary BEd courses devote a
substantial period of time to specialist subject studies, equivalent to
two years of a four-year course, together with six months geared to
the application of the subject specialism to primary teaching. PGCE
students will be expected to have covered their subject specialism
mainly through their first degree but the application of that subject
to teaching does form a significant part of the course. All courses
offer a grounding in the teaching of English, mathematics and
science – at least 150 hours per subject. Courses encourage students
to consider approaches to understanding how children learn and the
importance this has for teaching and curriculum organisation.
Other important aspects of courses include pupil assessment and
evaluation, classroom discipline, information technology, pastoral
responsibilities and the structure of the education service. See
Chapter 4 on routes into teaching for more details.

☐ SECONDARY EDUCATION

What is secondary education?
After primary education, pupils go on to secondary schools which
may be grammar, secondary modern, comprehensive or specialist
schools. Specialist schools comprise City Technology Colleges,
language colleges, specialist arts colleges and sports colleges. There
are approximately 4,000 secondary schools and around 160 of these
are grammar schools. Grammar schools select pupils on the basis of
academic ability. Secondary modern schools exist in areas operating
grammar schools and cater for those not selected. Comprehensive
schools cater for all pupils regardless of ability. However, even
comprehensive schools may organise pupils into classes streamed
according to ability. Others may have mixed ability classes, or a
combination of streaming and mixed ability depending on the
subject. All schools, including comprehensives, can select up to ten
per cent of pupils on ability and may apply to the Secretary of State
for Education if they want to increase this figure.

Secondary schools cater for pupils within the age group 11 to 18,
with pupils having the option to leave school at 16 once they have

completed their compulsory schooling. In some areas, secondary schools concentrate on the 11-16 age group. If a school does not have a sixth form, pupils leaving secondary schools at 16 have the option of continuing on to local colleges which may be sixth form, further education, technology, tertiary or specialist colleges.

What is taught in secondary schools?
Pupils in secondary schools are taught the National Curriculum subjects which include the core subjects – English (plus Welsh in Wales), mathematics and science and foundation subjects – history, geography, technology, music, art, PE and foreign languages. Some subjects such as English and mathematics are studied throughout this period; others such as art may be dropped at age 14. Pupils also study religious education. Between the ages of 14 to 16, pupils study for GCSEs (General Certificate of Secondary Education) in National Curriculum and other subjects. They have a degree of choice as to some of the subjects they take. Most GCSEs include a mixture of coursework and examinations and are graded from A*/A to G. They are compulsory for the majority of pupils and, once they have finished their GCSEs, pupils have completed their compulsory schooling and are free to leave school if they wish.

Alongside GCSEs, pupils may also be given the option of taking vocational courses such as City & Guilds and RSA qualifications, for example in computing, typing and word processing and Part One GNVQs (General National Vocational Qualifications).

GNVQs are available in a variety of work-related areas such as business studies, health and social care, leisure and tourism, science, engineering and others and are offered at three levels – Foundation, Intermediate and Advanced. Part One GNVQs have been specifically developed for pupils aged 14–16 and they are equivalent to half a GNVQ. Currently, a few selected schools are piloting Part One GNVQs in several vocational areas including business, health and social care, manufacturing, art and design, information technology and leisure and tourism. Other vocational areas may be added at a later date. Part One GNVQs are equivalent to two GCSEs and are offered at Foundation and Intermediate level. A Part One Foundation GNVQ is broadly comparable to two GCSEs at grades D–G and an Intermediate Part One is broadly equivalent to two GCSEs at grades A–C.

At 16, if pupils want to continue in education, they can either stay on in their school's sixth form, if it caters for the 16–18 age group, or go to a local college. Schools with sixth forms usually offer pupils the choice of a variety of courses including: GCE A levels and AS, repeat GCSEs, full GNVQs at Intermediate and Advanced level and other vocational courses awarded by City & Guilds, RSA and by Edexcel Foundation, BTEC.

A levels are available in a wide range of subject areas and are two year courses for which pupils are usually required to have achieved four or five GCSEs at grade A–C. A levels are graded from A to E. They can include some coursework but most still have an emphasis on examinations at the end of two years which test knowledge and understanding of the whole syllabus. In recent years, modular A level courses have been developed in which pupils take examinations regularly throughout the course. However, following the recommendations of Sir Ron Dearing's *Review of Qualifications for 16-19 Year Olds* (March 1996), it is likely that, in the future, all modular A level courses will include an end-of-course examination covering topics studied over the two years.

AS (Advanced Supplementary) qualifications, which are designed to be half the content of the full A level but at the same standard, are currently being reviewed. Following Dearing's recommendations, a new AS qualification may be introduced which will be renamed the Advanced Subsidiary (AS). The new AS will count as 40 per cent of an A level and will take one year to complete and will not be considered to be half an A level in terms of performance.

Schools offering GNVQs usually only offer a selected number of vocational areas. Pupils taking the Foundation level require no qualifications. For the Intermediate level, pupils usually need several GCSEs at grades D and E, or to have successfully completed a relevant Foundation GNVQ. The Advanced GNVQ is equivalent to two A levels and usually requires four or five GCSEs at grade A–C, or successful completion of a relevant Intermediate GNVQ. For further information on GNVQs, contact the National Council for Vocational Qualifications. You will find the address at the back of the book.

What do secondary teachers do?
Secondary teachers are specialists, teaching one or more of the National Curriculum subjects described elsewhere in this book or

vocational courses which can make up part of the school curriculum (usually for 14–16 year olds). However, teachers have other responsibilities as well as teaching their specialist subjects. Teaching involves a lot of administrative work, marking and lesson preparation, much of which takes place outside school hours.

Secondary teachers help their pupils pass through significant stages of their lives. Many pupils depend on teachers for advice on career choices and subject choices for examinations. As a secondary teacher you will also become involved with pupils through extra-curricular activities.

Teachers are expected to contribute to the development of the delivery of their subject in the school and, if you become head of a subject department, you will have to lead and manage a team of teachers.

You will also have to deal with a wide range of people. Parents are increasingly involved with schools as are local business representatives. You may also have to liaise with social workers, school inspectors and governors.

How do you train to work in secondary schools?
There is a wide variety of ways in which you can qualify to become a secondary teacher. The chapter on routes into teaching gives full details. (See page 41.)

Specialist schools
Some pupils attend one of the 196 specialist schools introduced since 1988. The 151 technology colleges, 15 city technology colleges and 30 language colleges provide secondary education through the National Curriculum. However, they also have an additional emphasis on mathematics, science, technology and languages. They maintain close links with employers such as British Aerospace, Glaxo Wellcome and the Hong Kong and Shanghai Bank group and receive funding from them as well as the Department for Education and Employment (DfEE).

☐ MANAGEMENT OF STATE SCHOOLS

The Government has given schools more freedom to make their own decisions, spend their own budgets and plan their own futures. In this way it is hoped that schools can take responsibility for achieving high standards and be accountable for their performance to parents and the local community. Self-government for schools can take the following forms.

Local Management of LEA Schools
Local Management of Schools (LMS) has given all LEA schools wide-ranging powers to manage their affairs. The school governors, perhaps comprising the head teacher, parents and members of the local community, make decisions about how to spend the budgets allocated to them by the local council on such things as salaries, heating and school buildings.

Grant-Maintained Schools
These are state schools that have 'opted out' of LEA control, through a ballot of the parents. They are run by the governors, rather than by the governors and the LEA. The governors take over the school, its buildings and plant. They are responsible for employing the staff and, together with the head teacher, for all aspects of management including in-service staff training. Over 1,000 of the 24,000 state schools have opted out of LMS to become grant-maintained schools but the opting out rate has recently slowed down dramatically.

☐ FURTHER EDUCATION INCLUDING SIXTH FORM COLLEGES

This sector includes sixth form colleges, tertiary colleges and colleges of Further Education. Courses are offered at different levels in many subjects including business, humanities, languages, education, science and technology, art and design and agriculture and horticulture.

Sixth form colleges are widely established in the country. They specialise in academic education for 16-19 year olds. Pupils can transfer to them at age 16 and study A levels, AS, GCSEs and GNVQs.

Tertiary colleges replaced traditional sixth forms and Further Education colleges in some areas of England and Wales. They offer the full range of academic and vocational courses or specialise in academic and vocational courses that cover a limited range of disciplines.

The Further Education sector is the main provider of post-16 education in the United Kingdom and has experienced significant growth in recent years. In England, for example, there was a 17 per cent increase in student numbers in FE colleges between 1994-5 and 1995-6, with over 3.5 million students studying at 450 colleges.

The last five years have seen a period of unprecedented changes in addition to the increase in student numbers. The sector is recognised as a major contributor to the achievement of the national education and training targets, and colleges in England, Wales and Scotland have been reconstituted as independent corporations, leading to a more entrepreneurial sector with intensified competition for students. Local Education Authorities have increasingly transferred responsibilities for their adult education provision to local FE institutions.

Colleges offer a range of full and part-time vocational and academic qualifications. They have become increasingly flexible in the hours of attendance, course content and level to allow a wider range of people to study.

Colleges are broadly similar across the United Kingdom and provision typically covers the following range:

Academic courses - Students take GCSEs, A levels, AS. Students may be taking GCSEs to improve their grades and adults may be taking A levels in preparation for university or simply out of interest. Colleges also offer access courses for mature students, usually validated by consortia of Higher and Further Education instititutions. Colleges are increasingly offering Higher Education courses. In 1996 this stood at 13 per cent of Higher Education courses in the UK, although the Association of Scottish Colleges calculated recently that more than a quarter of Scotland's Higher Education students are studying in Further Education colleges. Courses are run under a variety of arrangements; for example, franchise courses that deliver Higher Education courses through an FE college, or two-plus-two schemes where students take part of a Higher Education programme at an FE college and, if successful, move to a Higher Education institution to finish the course.

11

Vocational education - The main vocational option is the General National Vocational Qualification offered by examination bodies such as the City & Guilds of London Institute (CGLI), the Royal Society of Arts (RSA), the Business and Technician Education Council (BTEC). These and other examination boards, such as the London Chamber of Commerce and Industry (LCCI) also offer other vocational qualifications, from basic to advanced level covering business and secretarial courses, commercial courses and courses for industry.

Training for jobs - Colleges also offer National Vocational Qualifications (NVQs), skills-based qualifications that recognise and develop ability in a trade or profession. Around 600 NVQs are available in areas as various as aquatics, dry cleaning, book editing and building site management. Five levels are available ranging from Level 1 for competence in work activities which are mostly routine and predictable to Level 5, which shows competence in applying complex techniques in a wide range of contexts, often with significant responsibility for the work of others. While NVQs are essentially about training for work, colleges may offer NVQs by assessing candidates in workplace conditions.

Colleges also offer specialist certificated and short courses for people in work in a range of disciplines that have yet to become NVQ accredited.

Case Study: Lecturing at a Further Education college

Bernard Tannett lectures at a large inner city Further Education college. He started with the college as a part-time lecturer in 1986 without any formal teaching qualifications. 'I actually studied at this college for my A levels before taking a degree in history and politics and an MSc in politics and sociology. I came back to start an A level in economics and got chatting to my old lecturer and he offered me some part-time work teaching on a GCSE American studies.'

Bernard spent a number of years working on a temporary, part-time basis, building up the range of subjects he taught and, after five years, applied for and obtained a full-time lecturer post. 'I now teach GCSEs, A levels and a multi-disciplinary Access course that prepares students for humanities degrees in Higher

Education. I am teaching topics that interest me – World Powers, sociology, politics, American studies.'

'It is important to show enthusiasm', says Bernard, 'I was asked to teach GCSE World Powers, for example, a week before the course started and I was only a week ahead of my students for most of the course but this willingness helped get me established.' While this route into Further Education (Bernard still has no formal teaching qualification) is still possible, increasingly, the college recruits through a local PGCE Further Education institution. 'It's more difficult now to get permanent contracts and lecturers have to be flexible. I feel lucky because I have been able to shape my career towards Access courses but it's entirely possible that I could be asked to teach something like business studies, for example.'

During his time at the college Bernard has taken on a number of roles. 'I have been a subject leader, which involves managing the course, appointing part-time staff, deciding which exam papers to include and looking at the examination results. I have also been a course leader which is an even more demanding role - running the whole course provision, working out the tutorial programme, the structure of the course, enrolment, social events, discipline, pastoral matters and liasing with the Student Council. You get some reduction in teaching time with these jobs, but only two hours a week. In the early part of my teaching career I was doing 60 hour weeks.'

Bernard, still clearly enjoys teaching. 'Teaching interested people is a joy. My Access and A level politics students have a burning desire to learn but they aren't just having an education experience here, a lot of them are going through a life change. As a course tutor for Access I have to ensure we operate within guidelines set by the external moderators but we have a lot of freedom about what and how we teach. The course covers subjects such as politics, history, economics and English but content is really a vehicle to teaching study skills. How to write research notes and make essay plans, for example. Teaching is also part of my continuing learning. The A level politics course I take for three hours on Monday evenings has less freedom. The course has to be tightly structured and we can't afford leisurely discussions about New Labour, for example.'

*As well as teaching adults Bernard takes 16 and 17 year olds
through GCSE courses. 'My A level and Access courses have very
motivated, independent learners who can be intellectually
challenging but the GCSE students are 'second chancers',
students who are retaking exams to improve grades. Relatively,
it is less rewarding for the amount of effort you have to put in.'*

*Bernard has recently taken the decision to go part-time.
'Frankly, I did this to save my sense of vocation. There is a lot of
pressure in teaching. Colleges are increasingly market-driven.
Classes can be large and more teaching time is being demanded.
This can cut into your preparation time and makes marking and
assessment even more time consuming. Access students rightly
demand very detailed feedback but if each piece of work they
hand in takes twenty minutes to mark and you have a class of
twenty you can see the pressures building up.'*

See page 54 for information on training to teach in Further Education
and a case study on a PGCE in Further Education student and page
85 for a case study of a Further Education lecturer teaching English
as a second language.

☐ SPECIAL NEEDS PROVISION

What are special needs?
Around 20 per cent of school-age children are estimated to have
special educational needs at some point in their school career.
A child with special educational needs can be defined as one who, for
a number of reasons, is making significantly slower progress in one
or more areas of his or her development than others of the same age
group. These could include children who have temporary difficulties
with reading or writing or those with an accumulation of physical
and mental disabilities. The Royal National Institute for the Blind,
for example, estimates that 56 per cent of visually impaired children
have other disabilities such as physical, hearing, learning or
communication difficulties.

Learning difficulties may also be due to a range of physical and
medical conditions such as epilepsy, diabetes and cystic fibrosis;
emotional and behavioural difficulties or hyperactivity; dyslexia or
speech difficulties. The range of difficulties are often described in a
range from mild and moderate learning difficulty to severe, multiple
and profound learning difficulty. However, only two per cent of

children have special needs in the last category where the long-term, severe and complex nature of the difficulties require the provision of special schooling or additional resources.

Where are special needs children taught?
The 1981 Education Act changed the law regarding children with disabilities and special needs and stated that: 'Where possible, all children with special educational needs should be educated in ordinary schools' and 'For integration to be effective, pupils with special educational needs must be engaged in all or most of the activities of the school'. This includes, of course, access to the National Curriculum. The legal obligation on local education authorities (LEAs) to integrate children with special needs in mainstream schools is dependent on their parents' views being considered and also on integration being compatible with providing 'efficient education' for the other children in the school and the efficient use of resources. The Act gave a spur to those areas of the country that already had strong integration policies. All initial teacher training courses include at least an introduction to special educational needs, with a varying emphasis from course to course. Furthermore, all schools have a special educational needs teacher coordinator and a governor who will have responsibility for special education.

Special needs children are taught either in mainstream schools, special schools or special units attached to mainstream schools. The special schools may be LEA maintained or independent, offer boarding or day facilities and be mixed or single-sex. Schools may be oriented to a particular disability or aim to teach according to the severity of the learning difficulty. The promotion of integration means that special schools will, wherever possible, send pupils to mainstream schools, even if it is only for specific classes. Similarly, mainstream schools may arrange for their pupils to attend special schools. This form of partial integration may give special needs pupils their first experience of an ordinary classroom routine and promote understanding and caring in those who do not have special educational needs.

How do you become a special needs teacher?
Those who wish to teach children with special educational needs have first to obtain Qualified Teacher Status and obtain 'some' experience of teaching in a mainstream setting. The DfEE does not specify any additional training before taking up an appointment

teaching children with special needs. However, most teachers will be able to take part in specialist in-service training courses or postgraduate diplomas or master's degrees, usually after one or two years' mainstream experience. Courses may be provided by local education authorities or by teacher training institutions, after school hours or as part of whole school in-service training days. Courses offered by institutions dealing with serious disabilities may take place over many months. Courses may cover such things as the social and educational issues around the disability, the resources available for such pupils during school life and into adulthood, and the role of support services. Modules may, for example, cover the strategies for teaching the National Curriculum on behalf of the special needs group in question and offer an overview of teaching approaches and techniques in relation to the disability.

Those teaching visually impaired pupils in a special school or pupils with serious hearing impairments are obliged to successfully complete one of the special training courses approved by the DfEE relating to visual or sensory impairment within three years of taking up an appointment.

Many courses for special needs require mainstream experience from their participants but disability organisations are campaigning for teacher training to provide routes that would allow those who wish to do so to go straight from teacher training on to these specialist courses.

Case Study: Special educational needs teacher

Barbara is head teacher at Clapham Park School, a special needs school with 28 pupils in the age range from five to 16 years.

'Originally I trained for secondary teaching but moved away from it because its exam orientation stopped becoming a challenge. I began to find teaching low-achieving youngsters a much greater challenge – getting bright children through exams is relatively easy. Then, when my own children started primary school, I took much more of an interest in that sector and was able to move from secondary teaching into primary teaching. I attended a range of primary in-service training courses rather than the formal retraining courses which were available. My first job in a primary school involved me in integrating the

school's partially hearing youngsters into its mainstream classes.'

Barbara feels that a background in mainstream work gives special needs teachers the ability to measure the progress of their pupils against what is expected of normal children. 'Our integration policy facilitates this in that we are sending our pupils to the mainstream schools but, significantly, our teachers are teaching mainstream youngsters who come to our school on part-time placements.' Integration is not seen as benefiting only special needs pupils. 'Certainly it is good for our pupils – by extending their peer group, for example – but our mainstream partner schools like it as well,' says Barbara. 'We have smaller classes and often have better facilities.'

The gap between the mainstream and special schools has also been narrowed by other recent changes in education. 'The introduction of the National Curriculum has been good for the special needs sector,' says Barbara. 'It ensures our pupils an entitlement to a broad and balanced curriculum and moves away from the limited emphasis on care.' Students at Clapham Park take GCSEs as well as other accreditation such as Youth Awards. 'The GCSE papers, as such, make no allowances for special needs pupils and students with visual impairments can be disadvantaged simply because they cannot see the papers so well and take much longer to read them. We sometimes have to request that our pupils are exempted from certain papers, or ask for special consideration such as extra time. These arrangements can place extra pressure on our administration without any additional funding.'

As a head teacher Barbara is centrally involved with the appointment of new teachers. 'A proven interest and commitment to special needs education is obviously important but, before that, I need staff who have proved themselves to be good teachers, who understand how children learn and how teaching can be adapted to meet the needs of individual pupils. We often appoint teachers who have been trained for the primary sector and who have experience of dealing with pupils of below-average ability.'

Once in post teachers will certainly be expected to take advantage of the training available through the Local Education Authority

*or through initial teacher training institutions. These courses
may be short courses, BPhils, diplomas or the mandatory
courses required for those who are teaching visually impaired or
hearing impaired children. 'As a special school we expect staff to
take appropriate courses and we offer day release and in-school
support over the course of a year for the mandatory courses'.
Training in the special needs sector has been the focus of some
concern and a recent report by the Special Educational Needs
Training Consortium was commissioned by the Department for
Education and Employment. The report, published in March
1996, highlighted the fact that significant numbers of teachers
working with special needs pupils had not received appropriate
training and that, in some areas, the numbers of appropriately
trained teachers was falling. The number of teachers of the deaf
passing the mandatory course has been falling steadily since
1989 and the average age of those training to be teachers of the
deaf is now 40 years.*

*Barbara feels that the proposed changes in initial teacher
training (ITT) courses may give special needs training a higher
profile in the ITT curriculum. 'Training for special needs is
useful training for all teachers,' says Barbara. 'After all, what it
equips teachers to do above all is to appreciate the individual
needs of the pupil and to modify the teaching approach based on
that understanding.'*

☐ THE INDEPENDENT SECTOR

What is independent education?
Independent schools are schools which receive no direct income from
state sources. Their funding comes largely from fees paid by parents.
There are many types of independent schools – selective and non-
selective, boarding and day, large and small, mixed and single-sex,
urban and rural providing education for children aged from three
years to 18 years. Some independent schools have a religious
orientation with all the main Christian denominations having a
presence. Others have strong Jewish or Muslim links but there are
other schools which do not have any particular emphasis on religion.
There are about 2,500 independent schools in Great Britain,
educating more than seven per cent of the nation's children and 18
per cent of sixth formers. The Government's Assisted Places Scheme

for day children in independent schools at secondary and, from September 1997, preparatory level offers financial assistance for some pupils. However, the Labour government is committed to abolishing the Assisted Places Scheme. More than 25 per cent of pupils in independent schools now receive assistance with the payment of fees.

What is involved in teaching in independent schools?
This sector, in general, has schools with smaller class sizes and achieves some of the best examination results. A smaller number of schools offer vocational qualifications as well. Pre-preparatory schools teach pupils from age 4 and preparatory schools from ages 7 to 11 or 13. Pupils are drawn from across the ability range. Preparatory schools traditionally have prepared pupils for the entry requirements of independent senior schools but many of their pupils do go on to schools in the state-funded sector. In senior schools, pupils take GCSEs and virtually all go on to A-levels, allowing teachers the satisfaction of teaching their subject to a high level to well-motivated students. While independent schools are overwhelmingly oriented to academic qualifications, a growing number are also offering vocational qualifications such as Advanced GNVQs, particularly in Art and Design and Business Studies.

Independent schools have more flexibility than maintained schools in a number of important respects. There is no legal requirement, for example, for them to embrace the National Curriculum but most, in fact, do teach its content although they may have a different system for testing and assessment. There are some 'progressive' schools which emphasise dialogue between pupil and teacher without a rigid framework of regulations and conventions. Independent schools may also be less bound by external financial constraints; some pay above the national salary scales and have more freedom in the allocation of responsibility allowances. Teachers in independent schools do not necessarily have Qualified Teacher Status and some are appointed direct from university but the vast majority of teachers in independent schools will have a teaching qualification. Preparatory schools need secondary-trained as well as primary-trained teachers. Up to the age of nine, children are taught by class teachers but, after this, secondary-trained teachers with subject specialisms are increasingly used.

The ending of the formal probation period for newly qualified teachers removes a significant professional disadvantage for teachers starting their careers in independent schools – as long as the school provides an appropriate induction programme. Previously, teachers who had taught solely in independent schools were not permitted to teach in state schools. There is now a good deal of mobility between the independent and maintained sectors but it is entirely possible to make a career in independent schools only. In day schools promotion is via department and then whole school or divisional responsibility. In boarding schools (a smaller sector than previously) there are departmental and pastoral routes as, for example, head of a boarding house.

Montessori schools

There are around 800 Montessori schools in the UK following the 'indirect' teaching method defined by Dr Maria Montessori in 1907. It is called an indirect teaching method because the child is given freedom to grow and learn in a natural way but within a carefully planned and structured environment. Montessori schools cover an age range from nursery to age 12. Those who wish to teach in Montessori institutions will need to obtain an appropriate Montessori qualification – for more information see the address in Chapter 13.

Rudolf Steiner schools

There are a small number of Rudolf Steiner schools, named after their originator, the Austrian philosopher/educationalist, who founded his first school in 1919. Their educational philosophy stresses the importance of understanding the nature of childhood and the process of growth and this underpins the distinctive Steiner curriculum. Teaching in a Steiner school covers kindergarten and playgroups (three to six year olds), class teaching (seven to 14 year olds), upper school specialist teaching in two or more subjects for 14 to 18 year olds and specialist teaching throughout the school in languages, music, crafts, games and hand skills such as knitting and weaving and, eventually, woodwork and metalwork. Those wishing to teach in Steiner schools should be mature people, be committed to the Steiner philosophy and, ideally, have a degree or recognised teacher training qualification. In addition, applicants will need to take a Steiner accredited course. These vary in length from one year full-time to up to three years part-time.

How do you find a job in an independent school?
Independent schools recruit staff directly. The Times Educational
Supplement has a separate section for independent schools and some
schools also use specialist agencies. The Independent Schools
Information Service, set up by the Government-recognised
Independent Schools Joint Council, publishes a useful booklet
entitled *Teaching In Independent Schools* which offers further
guidance and information on working in the independent sector.

☐ THE SCOTTISH EDUCATION SYSTEM

What is the Scottish education system?
The Scottish education system is unique and there are many
differences between teaching in Scotland and in England and Wales
or Northern Ireland.

Around 96 per cent of pupils attend schools which are comprehensive,
co-educational, and provided free of charge by 32 local authorities.
Only a small number of schools have 'opted out'. School provision is
also available through the independent schools which offer both day
and boarding places for pupils of school age.

The Scottish Qualifications Authority
The Scottish Qualifications Authority (SQA) is responsible for most
types of qualification in Scotland. These range from the Standard
Grade, Higher Grade and National Certificate Modules that almost
all school pupils take, to Higher National Certificates (HNCs),
Higher National Diplomas (HNDs) and Scottish Vocational
Qualifications (SVQs). The SQA is also responsible for 5-14
Assessment in schools.

Primary schooling: 5-12 years
Primary schools take pupils from age five to 12 years. Classes
contain both boys and girls and cover the full range of abilities; there
is no selection or streaming by ability. The approach to teaching
reflects this with a mixture of whole-class, group and individual
pupil techniques. The use of group methods is particularly
characteristic and trains the pupils to work co-operatively as well as
independently, following a programme set out by the class teacher.
Curriculum integration is also an important approach followed in

primary schools; linking different curricular areas or subjects to each other by means of project work, generally of an environmental studies nature.

There is no National Curriculum as such but the Scottish curriculum is delivered in a framework set by The Scottish Office Education and Industry Department (SOEID). From the age of five to 14, education focuses on five areas:
language
mathematics
religious, moral and social education
expressive arts
environmental studies.

The class teacher is expected to be able to teach all aspects of the curriculum but may well receive support from visiting teachers of art, drama, music and physical education.

Lower secondary schooling: 12–16 years.
Secondary schooling sets out to provide an education which prepares pupils for a place in society and meets their personal, social and vocational needs, the expectations of their parents, of employers and of tertiary education. For the first two years of secondary schooling all pupils undertake a common course with a wide range of subjects, some of which are new to the pupils. Typical subjects such as English, mathematics, a modern foreign language and science (which have to be studied up to age 16) can be augmented by subjects such as media studies, business studies and Gaelic. Towards the end of the second year pupils choose courses for years three and four of secondary schooling. These are taken from a menu of 'core' subjects and an optional element (about 25–30% of the time available). Culminating in the Scottish Certificate of Education, Standard Grade. This certificate is gained by examination with an element of assessment within the school itself.

From secondary year three up to secondary year six pupils may also take short courses in subjects such as electronics, Latin and statistics, designed to be taught in a maximum of 40 hours. Each short course is free-standing but combinations of courses may be linked to a programme of study in a particular area. Assessment of short courses is internal, with external moderation by the Scottish Qualification Authority. Successfully completed short courses are reported on the Scottish Certificate of Education.

Pupils in secondary years three and four can also take vocational qualifications and by completing them successfully receive credit towards the National Certificate which is a 'non-advanced' vocational qualification. The four years of lower secondary schooling normally culminate in the Scottish Certificate of Education Standard Grade. The examination is structured in such a way that almost all pupils in the age group take the examination. Results are reported on a scale of 1 - 7, with 1 the highest, in a profile of performance which gives grades for parts of each subject (elements) as well as an overall award. For example, in English, separate element grades are reported for Reading, Writing and Talking as well as for the subject as a whole.

Upper Secondary School Education: 16-18 years
This stage involves vocational training and preparation for Higher Education. All 16 year olds must be given two weeks of work experience in local firms as part of their general pre-vocational training. Pupils may study the same subjects as in previous years but at a higher level. Culminating in the Higher Grade of the Scottish Certificate of Education taken usually in no more than five subjects. A wide variety of subjects are available including Accounting and finance, chemistry, management and information studies, Spanish and technological studies. These certificates are the target for many school pupils who aim to enter professions or to go into Higher Education.

Another certificate, the Certificate of Sixth Year Studies (CSYS) is for candidates in the sixth year of secondary school education. Awards at CSYS are not always necessary for university entrance but are a valuable additional qualification, as these courses help students to develop independent study methods and include self-directed project and investigative work. A Higher Grade pass or equivalent in the subject concerned is a necessary requirement to be presented for a CSYS course.

From August 1998 a new system of courses and qualifications is proposed which will affect post-16 education. The development will build on the Standard Grade enabling pupils in Secondary years 3 and 4 to choose courses in the knowledge that there are appropriate programmes for them to go on to.

The current Higher and Certificate of Sixth Year Studies will be revised and additional courses provided at levels between Standard Grade and Higher. After completion of Standard Grade in Secondary year 4 there will be five levels of courses available in Secondary 5 and 6 provisionally called Foundation, General, Credit, Higher and Advanced Higher. The proposed new Higher matches the current Higher and the Advanced Higher is intended to match the current Sixth Year Studies course.

In each subject area - including academic and vocational subjects - there will be five level patterns of courses enabling all students to study at an appropriate level. This pattern of courses will also apply at Further Education college level. Students will be able to take a mix of subjects at different levels but the level which they take in the Secondary fifth year will be determined by the level they reach at Standard Grade.

As well as the units that make up the courses students have opportunities for assessment and certification of core skills in communication, numeracy, problem solving, personal and interpersonal skills, and information technology.

There is a Guide to Education and Training in Scotland on the Internet at http://www.ed.ac.uk/~riu/GETS/

Other Scottish qualifications
The SQA provides a number of additional vocational and academic qualifications.

National Certificate Modules
Four out of five secondary pupils also take at least one module from the range of 3000 vocational modules - from accountancy to welding. They are also a popular choice at colleges and adult training centres.

Clusters
National Certificate Clusters are coherent packages of modules requiring more detailed knowledge in areas such as European Studies, Information Technology and Home Economics. They have been introduced to help candidates make relevant choices from the vast range of National Certificate Modules.

General Scottish Vocational Qualifications (GSVQs)
Also known as National Certificate Group Awards, these are broad-

based qualifications constructed from groups of related modules. They are designed mainly for 16 - 19 year olds in schools and colleges and for adults returning to education. They give candidates a wide range of skills relevant to employment and have clear links with Scottish Vocational Qualifications (SVQs).

An important part of each award is the development and assessment of core skills such as numeracy and communication, fundamental skills that employers regard as essential for almost all occupations.

Scottish Vocational Qualifications
Scottish Vocational Qualifications (SVQs) are designed to be delivered in the workplace and are based on national standards developed by employers themselves. There are over 800 SVQs, covering most occupations at all levels.

Higher National Certificates and Diplomas (HNCs and HNDs)
Offered by colleges, some universities and many other training centres, HNCs and HNDs are specially designed to meet the needs of employers both locally and nationally. Because of this, they are highly valued by employers seeking staff at higher technician or junior management level, whilst they are also recognised by many professional and technical bodies. Many HNCs and HNDs are regarded as being equivalent to the first or second year of a degree course. In fact, successful candidates can often transfer directly in to the latter stages of a degree course at a university. More than 1000 courses are on offer in popular areas like Business Administration, Information and Office Management, Travel and Tourism, and Engineering as well as in Broadcasting, Agriculture, Computing and Craft subjects.

The SQA can be contacted at:
Hanover House
24 Douglas Street
Glasgow
G2 7NQ
Scotland
Telephone: 0141 248 7900
Fax: 0141 242 2244
Email: mail@sqa.org.uk

They also have a Web site at www.sqa.org.uk/

How do you qualify to teach in Scotland?
To work as a teacher in education authority schools in Scotland, you must have a teaching qualification and be registered with the General Teaching Council for Scotland.

Teaching qualifications are awarded on successful completion of a teacher education course. Entry requirements for courses are defined in terms of Scottish Certificate of Education (SCE) awards and passes. Equivalent qualifications are also acceptable.

Registration and the probationary period
Once qualified, teachers register with the General Teaching Council for Scotland. As a new teacher you will take a two-year probationary period before becoming eligible for full registration. Final registration is granted subject to recommendation by a head teacher.

How do you qualify as a primary teacher in Scotland?
There are two courses available:

*   a four-year BEd
*   a one-year PGCE.

Minimum entry requirements for a BEd are SCE Higher grade passes in at least three subjects (one of which must be English) and Standard Grade awards (Grades 1–3) in two other subjects. A pass in mathematics at either level must be included.

Minimum entry requirements for the PGCE are a degree, a SCE Higher Grade pass in English, and a SCE Standard Grade (Grades 1–3) in mathematics.

Those entering in the year 2000 will need mathematics at Standard Grade Credit Level (Grades 1 or 2) for both the BEd and the PGCE.

How do you qualify as a secondary teacher in Scotland?
A Teaching Qualification (TQ) in Secondary Education is awarded in a particular subject or subjects of the secondary school curriculum after completion of one of the following courses in a teacher education college:

*   a four-year BEd in PE, music or technological education
*   a combined degree which includes subject study, study of

education and school experience
- a one-year PGCE following a degree.

TQs can be awarded in various subjects ranging from agriculture to Gaelic, English, physics and science. It is possible to attain a TQ in more than one subject.

Entry requirements for a BEd (secondary) course include:

- the requirements specified by the individual college
- SCE Higher Grade pass in English.

Those on the combined degree route also have to meet the SCE Higher Grade pass in English requirement but this can be obtained at any time before entry to the teacher education part of the course.

Entry requirements for a PGCE (secondary) course include:

- a degree with considerable emphasis (a total of at least two years) on at least two subjects to be taught in secondary school
- SCE Higher Grade pass in English.

The authoritative guide to entry requirements to courses is found in the annual *Memorandum on Entry Requirements to Courses of Teacher Education in Scotland* available from HMSO book shops.

Applications for PGCE courses are made through TEACH, the Teacher Education Admissions Clearing House. Forms have to be returned to TEACH between 1 September and 15 December of the year prior to entry.

Admission for degree courses of teacher education is through UCAS.

See the useful addresses section on page 87 for contact details.

☐ THE NORTHERN IRELAND EDUCATION SYSTEM

What is the Northern Ireland Education System?
Education in Northern Ireland is managed centrally by the

Department of Education for Northern Ireland (DENI) and locally by five Education and Library Boards (loosely equivalent to Local Education Authorities). While all schools are open to pupils regardless of religious background the traditional segregation of primary and post-primary education has been a distinctive feature of the education system.

The main categories of the 1300 schools in Northern Ireland are:

Controlled Schools - covering primary and secondary and provided by the Education and Library Boards. Attended mainly by Protestant children

Voluntary grammar schools - secondary schools which may have either Roman Catholic or non-denominational management. Caters for 11-18 year olds

Integrated schools - Over 30 new schools and a number of Controlled Schools at both primary and secondary level which aim to provide education for Roman Catholic and Protestant children together.

Voluntary maintained schools - Owned by trustees and mainly Roman Catholic or non-denominational. Some schools in this sector teach the curriculum through the Irish language medium

The curriculum
Schools follow a common curriculum based on six broad areas of study - English, mathematics, science and technology, the environment and society, creative and expressive studies and (for secondary and Irish-medium primary schools) language studies.

The curriculum is defined in terms of four key stages covering the 12 years of compulsory schooling

Key Stage 1, covers school years 1-4 for pupils aged 4 to 8 years
Key Stage2, covers school years 5-7 for pupils aged 9 to 11 years
Key Stage 3, covers school years 8-10 for pupils aged 12 to 14 years
Key Stage 4, covers school years 11-12 for pupils aged 15 to 16 years

At Key Stage 1/2 the curriculum is modulated through four educational themes - Education for Mutual Understanding, Cultural Heritage, Health Education and Information Technology. At Key Stage 3/4 two more themes, Economic Awareness and Careers

Education, are added. Transfer from primary to secondary takes place at 11 years. If pupils wish to attend a grammar school, they must sit two transfer tests in English, Mathematics and Science.

Further Education
There are 17 colleges of Further Education offering a wide range of vocational and non-vocational courses. The colleges are run by the Education and Library Boards but will become incorporated in 1997.

Higher Education
Almost half of school leavers go to some form of post-school education, more than 20 per cent of these study at university. Northern Ireland has two universities, The Queens University and The University of Ulster which has four campuses across Northern Ireland. In addition to the universities which offer PGCE courses there are two teacher training centres - St. Mary's College and Stranmillis College.

Teacher Training in Northern Ireland
Everyone who graduated after 1973 must have a teacher training qualification in order to gain a permanent teaching post in Northern Ireland primary or secondary schools. Applications for the BEd courses at Northern Ireland's universities have to be made through UCAS. Applications for the PGCE courses are made to the individual institutions listed below. Further details on application procedures is given in Teacher Training in Northern Ireland available from the teacher training institutions

Availability of places in Northern Ireland
The number of places in Northern Ireland is substantially greater for postgraduate secondary school teacher training than for primary school teacher training. Around 350 secondary places at Queens University and the University of Ulster and around 60 primary places at St Mary's and Stranmillis teacher training colleges. Stranmillis includes around 12 places for intending educational pyschologists.

The contact details are as follows:

The Queen's University
Belfast
BT9 1NN
Telephone 01232 245311

Offering Economics, English, IT, Mathematics, Languages, Politics, Religious Studies, Sciences, Social Sciences, (History and Geography as subsidiary subjects only. Secondary.

University of Ulster at Coleraine
Cromore Road,
Coleraine,
BT52 1SA
Telephone 01232 44141
Offering English with Theatre Studies, History, Geography, Art, Music. (Also offers Secondary Art and Design - apply via GTTR). Secondary.

University of Ulster (Jordanstown Campus)
Shore Road
Newton Abbey
BT37 0QB
Telephone 01232 365131
Offering Home Economics, Sport and Leisure Studies and Technology. Secondary.

St Mary's College
191 Falls Road
Belfast
BT12 6FE
Telephone 01232 327 678
Primary

Stranmillis College
Stranmillis
Belfast,
BT 5 5DY
Telephone 01232 381271
Primary

Teaching in Further Education in Northern Ireland
A teaching qualification is not mandatory for appointment to posts in Further Education. However, all new entrants to full-time permanent teaching or associate lecturer posts appointed after September 1994 without either a BEd or a PGCE have to pass the PGCE in Further and Higher Education offered by the University of Ulster.

This chapter is about the National Curriculum in England and Wales and gives a description of the core and foundation National Curriculum subjects (and, in addition, religious education which is an essential part of the basic curriculum) taught in state primary and secondary schools and in many independent schools. Those wishing to apply for teacher training courses will need to become familiar with the framework of the National Curriculum through further reading. The complete National Curriculum is available on the Internet (http://www.dfee.gov.uk/nc/) or as a book or floppy disc at £25 from The Stationery Office, PO Box 276, London SW8 5DT, telephone 0171 873 9090.

The Scottish and Northern Ireland education systems are significantly different and are covered in separate sections.

☐ THE NATIONAL CURRICULUM

The National Curriculum in England and Wales is followed in all state schools by pupils aged 5–16. It consists of three core subjects: English (plus Welsh in Wales), mathematics and science, plus seven foundation subjects: history, geography, technology, music, art, PE and for secondary pupils only, foreign languages. The current National Curriculum has been slimmed down to allow room for other subjects such as sociology, psychology and classics as well as vocational subjects, especially General National Vocational Qualifications (GNVQs). In addition, all schools teach religious education.

Pupils are tested in each subject at the ages of seven, 11 and 14. Legislation was announced in October 1996 that will ensure that pupils are given 'baseline' assessments at age five. Many schools and LEAs already carry out their own schemes but the Schools Curriculum and Assessment Authority is now advising the Secretary of State for Education and Employment on the best way to introduce a national approach. Some subjects such as English are studied throughout this period, others such as art may be dropped at age 14.

At present, modern foreign languages are taught from the age of 11 as part of the National Curriculum but some primary schools offer French to younger pupils.

KEY STAGES AND PUPILS' AGES

	Key Stage 1 Aged 5–7	Key Stage 2 Aged 7–11	Key Stage 3 Aged 11–14	Key Stage 4 Aged 14–16
English	█	█	█	█
Mathematics	█	█	█	█
Science	█	█	█	█
Physical education	█	█	█	█
Design & technology	█	█	█	█
Information technology	█	█	█	█
Modern foreign language			█	█
History	█	█	█	
Geography	█	█	█	
Music	█	█	█	
Art			█	

The National Curriculum is divided into four 'key' stages. Key Stage 1 takes pupils from 5–7 and Key Stage 4 covers ages 14–16. As well as the National Curriculum pupils study Religious Education and may take vocational courses such as GNVQs. Below you will find a brief description of each National Curriculum subject.

Core subjects

English

English is so important that it is studied by all pupils between the ages of five and 16. The National Curriculum aims to develop the reading, writing, speaking and listening skills of every child. Recent reports indicating that teenagers' writing skills are on the slide, that pupils are arriving at secondary schools struggling to read textbooks and use dictionaries and that more is being learnt about grammar in foreign language classes than in English lessons means that the work of English teachers will continue to be closely scrutinised. English teaching is not simply about reading and writing. The work involves a wide range of activities. Set texts will certainly include the classics such as Dickens and Shakespeare, for example, but also non-literary pieces and other books. It involves the development of good standards of spelling and handwriting along with the development of verbal communication skills through debates and talks.

At primary level English is taught by class teachers who have the vital task of developing pupils' reading skills. At secondary level teachers are involved in GCSE English, AS and A level. In addition, there may be duties as a form tutor and involvement in extra-curricular activities such as helping with the rehearsals for the school play.

Mathematics

Mathematics is a core curriculum subject for pupils aged between five and 16 and mathematics teachers are in great demand. The traditional textbook and exercise book approach to teaching is being transformed by a wider repertoire of exciting, interesting and relevant ways of tackling this discipline. Teachers use computers, videos and other equipment to investigate the subject.

Teachers need to be able to work with a wide variety of abilities and be able to inspire pupils to investigate and solve problems rather than simply downloading knowledge. Many mathematics teachers speak of the satisfaction to be obtained in helping those who are struggling with basic concepts as well as taking able sixth formers through A levels.

Science

There is a continuing demand for science teachers. It is a core subject in the school curriculum and is studied by all pupils in maintained schools up to age 16. The National Curriculum covers all the main elements of science: physics, chemistry, biology and earth sciences and astronomy together with work on the history and nature of science. Schools may design their own approach to delivering the subject – taking the three sciences separately or adopting a modular or integrated approach. The new system draws together strands of science that are common to the three major disciplines and ensures students are given a broad foundation before becoming more specialised. Science teachers work closely together in multi-disciplinary teaching teams.

Science teachers can expect to teach GCSEs, AS and A levels and GNVQs. As well as teaching your own science specialism, you will be encouraged to develop knowledge and skills in other related subject areas. Those with a biology background, for example, may need to do some in-service retraining in physical science to ensure they can contribute effectively to other sciences. This will be especially important for those hoping to take on departmental responsibilities.

Foundation subjects

Physical education (PE)

The status of PE in schools has been raised by its inclusion as one of the National Curriculum foundation subjects; it is studied by all pupils aged between five and 16. PE teachers have the responsibility for promoting physical competence and laying the foundations for a healthy lifestyle for a wide range of pupils with different interests and abilities. The emphasis is on participation across various activities including, individual and team games, athletics and gymnastics, swimming, and outdoor and adventurous pursuits. As well as participation, there has to be preparation and evaluation of activities.

At secondary level, PE teachers are responsible for delivering GCSEs in Physical Education and A levels in Sports Science which include written work and examinations and covers areas such as physiology, hygiene and sports psychology. There are also vocational courses in sports science and recreation and leisure and tourism which may require the input of PE teachers.

Many PE teachers teach other, academic, subjects as well as their specialism. Primary school teachers in any case teach the range of National Curriculum subjects including PE. Secondary level PE teachers can combine PE with teaching anything from biology to mathematics depending on their interests and abilities. It is advisable for PE teachers to be able to offer a second subject.

Technology

Technology is a foundation subject taught to all pupils aged five to 16 years. It combines a number of linked disciplines – craft, design and technology (CDT), art and design, business studies, home economics and information technology (IT). It also has strong links with other subject areas, particularly science and mathematics. Schools have a lot of flexibility as to how they deliver the subject. Much of the classroom work is project-based and will combine several different technology disciplines. A project on building a housing cooperative would involve discussions on materials and costs, construction methods and how different members of the cooperative would be involved. Computer design may be carried out and models may be created. Other work may involve projects such as designing a garden for the disabled, making a rocket launcher, designing jewellery boxes. Pupils may study to GCSE, A level/AS standard and vocational courses.

The cross-curricular approach involves technology teachers working closely with those of other disciplines.

Those wishing to become specialist technology teachers will need an appropriate first degree in engineering, design or architecture, for example, followed by a PGCE or to combine technology or a related specialism with a BEd or a BA/BSc carrying QTS. Other routes such as the School Centred Initial Teacher Training (SCITT) scheme may also be appropriate. For more details on this, see the next chapter.

Modern foreign languages

British Airways has recently been obliged to recruit from overseas to obtain bilingual cabin staff and a survey by recruitment consultants found that many UK jobs are being filled with bilingual candidates from France, Germany and the Benelux countries. News reports such as these have underlined why the Government has made modern foreign languages (MFL) one of the foundation subjects of the National Curriculum. In maintained schools the subject is taught from age 11 to 16 with students studying at least one and sometimes two languages. Britain's role in the European Union means that many pupils will study languages such as German, Spanish, Italian and French. The Government is also concerned to see a diversification from the traditional emphasis on French and the list of acceptable languages taught in schools as part of the National Curriculum includes Bengali, Hindi, Japanese, Arabic, Mandarin as well as other European languages.

The way languages are taught has also changed with an increased emphasis on the use of 'authentic' and relevant materials which will stimulate pupils, for example, making use of television programmes, newspapers and even railway timetables in the target language. Grammar remains an important issue, however, and students are taught how a language functions and how it is formed but with an emphasis on learning to use the language in realistic contexts.

Given the prevalence of English in the world, motivation for learning languages is a key issue for teachers. Since September 1996, schools have also had the option of offering free-standing GNVQ Language Units which will offer an alternative way of satisfying the National Curriculum modern foreign language requirements at Key Stage 4. Teachers have to keep abreast of the National Curriculum and GCSE requirements which change periodically. Language teachers are expected to conduct the whole of their class in the target language – greeting pupils and managing classroom activities in the language being studied.

In England and Wales, foreign languages are taught at secondary level but their introduction into primary is a current topic of national interest. In Scotland, because secondary education begins a year later, foreign languages are now usually covered in the later stages of the primary curriculum.

Those teaching languages will find that extra-curricular activities are an important part of their work. Language exchanges or work-shadowing visits are an important feature of learning languages.

Applicants wishing to teach modern foreign languages have to offer at least one language to a high level. Many will have studied it to degree level or at least taken it as part of a joint degree. Interviews will, in part, be conducted in the chosen language and applicants will need to be fluent for general communication purposes. Many applicants now offer a second language – not usually to the same level but possibly to A level standard, for example. Strong candidates often speak the language because it is their mother tongue. In a situation where schools are endeavouring to offer diversity and are also operating within tight budgets, applicants for jobs who can offer a high proficiency in a mother tongue coupled with another foreign language are much more employable than those able to offer only one language.

Unsurprisingly, given Britain's traditional weakness in languages, the subject is considered a 'shortage' subject and may attract additional funding through the Priority Subject Recruitment Scheme. Given the demand for language skills, this is likely to remain the case, particularly as applications for language degrees at UK universities are declining.

Those wishing to teach foreign languages may be interested in the following initiatives:

- *Joint PGCE / Maitrise Francais Langue Etrangere.*
This full-time, one year course enables students to qualify to teach French in the UK through the PGCE. The Maitrise Francais Langue Etrangere element of the course is taken in France and qualifies students to teach French as a Foreign Language to young people and adults in parts of the French education system. The UK institutions involved are Homerton College, Cambridge, University College of St. Martin, Kent, and the University of Nottingham. Applications are through the GTTR.

- *Lingua Assistants Programme.*
This programme sponsored by the European Commission is designed to promote the teaching and learning of foreign languages and strengthen the European dimension in the curriculum in schools and colleges. It involves the appointment of prospective teachers as assistants in other EU and member states for periods between three and eight months. Apply through the Central Bureau for Educational Visits and Exchanges. Contact details in the further information section on page 88.

History

History is a foundation subject for all pupils between the ages of five and 14. Between the ages of 14 and 16 pupils may study either history or geography or a combination of both subjects. History has an important place in the curriculum helping pupils to understand the present through the context of the past and helping to explain their own cultural roots. Because its key elements cover politics, economics, technological and scientific developments, social and religious matters it can contribute to a number of cross-curricular themes.

History teachers are expected to help pupils develop an awareness of the past and to understand why it differs from the present day. Younger pupils are brought to an understanding of the difference between myths, fairy tales and real historical events. The subject is brought alive by the use of real historical sources rather than textbooks alone. These can include cartoons, pictures and other materials. Visits may be arranged to historical sites or museums. British history obviously forms a major part of teaching, with a different emphasis in the different parts of the UK, but developments in other parts of Europe and the world are studied as well.

Geography

Geography is a foundation subject in the National Curriculum which means it is studied by all pupils between the ages of five and 14. Between 14 and 16 pupils study either History or Geography or a combination of both subjects. Guidelines are designed to ensure that pupils gain insights into the changing world and gain useful skills such as map-reading. Students are given a balanced grounding in physical, human and environmental geography. Fieldwork and enquiry are the basic approaches employed. Teachers may arrange visits to development sites to organise a project on, for example, energy conservation. Geography is a very interdisciplinary subject. It has links with other subjects in the curriculum including English and mathematics – through the use of maps, measurements and calculations; science; and history – with the search for explanations of how places and environments change over time.

Music

The introduction of music as a National Curriculum foundation subject has meant that, for the first time ever, it is compulsory for all pupils aged from five to 14. Music is available as a GCSE and an A level subject and can be taken in the context of vocational qualifications such as a GNVQ in Performing Arts and Entertainment Industries. This raised profile for music has helped create a national shortage of music teachers.

Music teaching has moved away from the traditional techniques of theory and music appreciation to a practical emphasis which encourages pupils to compose and to write down and record music and to perform, both individually and in groups. The range of music involved is very wide with music from different cultures and times, as well as more contemporary British music.

Music can be taught in classroom groups, through bands, choirs and school productions and through instrumental tuition to individuals and groups. Nursery, infant and junior classes are often taught by classroom teachers, who are not usually music specialists, and they depend very much on the support of the teacher acting as the school's music coordinator. School concerts, assemblies and choirs may also involve teachers or music coordinators. In secondary schools, music teachers may conduct choirs, orchestras, school productions and organise the visits of instrumental teachers.

Despite the minimum standards for music laid down by the National Curriculum, the provision of music teaching can be variable. Many schools have to ask parents to pay contributions towards instrumental teaching and the presence of choirs and orchestras depends on the commitment of individual teachers and the availability of funds.

Art and Design

Art and Design is a foundation subject within the National Curriculum which means it is a compulsory subject for all pupils up to age 14. After this age pupils may continue to study it up to GCSE or A level standard. In primary schools, teachers are able to use the delight children have in drawing, painting and making things from observation, memory and imagination to develop creativity and visual awareness. New technology is also being used alongside traditional block printing and model-making forms of art. In secondary schools, it is usually taught in studios by specialist teachers. Skills and disciplines include painting and drawing, print-making, computer-aided design, textiles, fashion, ceramics, photography and video. The National Curriculum also emphasises critical studies and pupils will need to be encouraged to discuss artists' use of colour and the statements artists were trying to make in particular works of art.

Religious Education (RE)

While RE is an essential component of the basic curriculum and compulsory for all pupils, including 14–16 year olds, there is no nationally prescribed framework of study and it is not formally part of the National Curriculum. The subject is taught according to syllabuses and targets agreed on a local basis with organisations such as the local education authority, governing bodies and local faith groups.

RE explores religions, their beliefs and practices, their place in different world cultures and how they shape personal ideas, values and behaviour. RE teachers need to be sympathetic to many different points of view as well as having a good knowledge of their subject. They do not necessarily need a personal faith although many

RE teachers do have such a foundation to their work. RE is not about seeking converts but is concerned with helping pupils appreciate the spiritual dimension and introduce such 'big' questions as 'Why am I here?' and 'How can I be happy?'

At primary level, RE is one of the subjects that class teachers take but those with a strong interest in the subject might aim to become the RE coordinator within their school. At secondary level, RE teachers teach a range of age groups and prepare pupils for GCSE and A level.

Chapter Four
ROUTES INTO TEACHING

The routes into teaching used to be fairly simple. School-leavers traditionally took a four-year BEd and graduates took a one-year Post Graduate Certificate in Education. Recently, in response to the more complex structure of education, and as a way of encouraging more entrants, many additional routes have become available. This section outlines the different routes available and for whom they may be appropriate.

Bachelor of Education (BEd)
Four-year full-time Bachelor of Education (BEd) courses are primarily for people who wish to train as primary teachers but there are a few courses geared to those wishing to teach in secondary schools, mainly in shortage subject areas. Courses are listed in the UCAS (Universities and Colleges Admissions Service) *Handbook*. If you train to teach in one sector and later wish to switch, from primary to secondary, for example, you may be able to take part-time or distance learning conversion courses. However, you will need to gain around two years of solid teaching experience before contemplating this. Four-year BEd courses include 32 weeks in the classroom and have a distinct emphasis on a specialist subject. The BEd is the most popular route into primary teaching. Apply via UCAS.

Case Study: A four-year BEd primary course
Jonathan Legon has just completed a successful first year as a teacher after taking a BEd in primary teaching at the University of North London. Jonathan works in a primary school in Hackney, London, which is successfully implementing special measures recommended by OFSTED, the government's inspection body.

Before deciding to become a teacher, Jonathan had spent a number of years in banking. He eventually gave this up and, after saving up enough money through working as a dispatch rider, he travelled the world. 'I never realised you could go to university without A levels,' says Jonathan, 'but after coming back from my trip I was really

*interested in becoming a teacher and made enquiries about training.'
At first Jonathan considered taking an Access course but quickly
realised that his Institute of Banking exams could be taken into
account for direct entry to the BEd course. 'I hadn't got a lot of
experience of working with kids,' says Jonathan, 'but I knew I had an
affinity with them from the way I got on with my nephews and nieces.
I made sure I knew what I was getting into by spending quite a few
weeks helping out in a local primary school. This turned out to be
really helpful because the head teacher gave me a really good
reference.'*

*While primary teachers have to teach the whole of the curriculum,
they are also expected to take a lead role in a specialist subject and
support other teachers within the school. 'I chose a BEd that offered
health, physical education and recreation as a main subject but I am
now teaching everything including mathematics and geography.' The
most difficult part of the BEd was not the academic work, which
included a 10,000-word dissertation in the final year as well as
blocks of teaching practice in different local schools, but surviving
financially. 'I took out several different loans but had to revert to
dispatch riding to keep my finances in shape. I guess other people
would have found different difficulties. I was lucky, for example, in
being able to concentrate on my work at home and not have to deal
with bringing up a family. After previously working 12-hour days as
a dispatch rider, setting aside some time every day for study wasn't
that difficult. 'Teaching practice is often an especially intense time for
trainee teachers but Jonathan, while finding it hard work, enjoyed it.
'The school arranged an amount of support, with a mentor, and my
tutor was also helpful. He used to be a school inspector and was able
to give me some good tips. However, despite all the support most of
the learning takes place in the classroom.'*

*After the course, Jonathan did not find it that difficult to get a job.
'Schools I hadn't heard of were phoning me up but I wanted to work
in London. A colleague from the course told me that Hackney was a
good place to work and recommended this school to me.' Jonathan
was not swayed by the bad press that Hackney, and other inner
London schools, receive. 'I have a class of 27 wonderful kids, whose
parents really care for them and who always turn up for school
events. The school does not lay down rigid rules about how I teach,
either. I have taught in small groups, which is very exhausting, and I
do some more traditional all-class teaching. The school does not
mind, as long as what I do works. I have really enjoyed my first year,*

particularly taking pupils from the stage where they were having real difficulties with mathematics, counting on the fingers of a hand, to where they were really achieving. One girl was really pleased because she knew she was making her dad happy.' Jonathan's experience of both his BEd and his first year in school has been very positive and he acknowledges that others may not be so fortunate. 'They may not be so lucky with their tutors at college or find a school like mine but it really has been fantastic.'

Three-year full-time BEd with or without Honours
Three-year BEd courses tend to be six-subject generalist primary degrees with less emphasis on a specialist subject than the four-year BEd and less opportunity for extended study at the highest level. As they have to cover much of the four-year BEd courses in a shorter time-scale, entry requirements may be more demanding. Three-year BEd courses include 24 weeks in the classroom. Some courses offer a general primary BEd after three years and a subject-specific BA or BSc with QTS after an extra year. There are still relatively few institutions offering this route and it is still too new to gauge employers' reactions to it. Apply via UCAS.

Shortened two-year full-time BEd
A two-year BEd is offered in shortage secondary subjects including mathematics, modern languages, physics, chemistry, music and design and technology. A small number of courses are also offered in the primary sector, particularly for overseas-trained teachers. Applicants must have completed at least a year of Higher Education (eg HND, HNC) in an appropriate subject area. Some institutions accept work experience instead of Higher Education as long as the work has involved a high degree of numeracy – accountancy and IT-based jobs are good examples. Apply via UCAS.

Three/four-year full-time BA/BSc with QTS
This degree qualifies people to teach but has more emphasis on subject specialisms. The main teaching practice tends to take place later in the course but students get some early exposure to schools work and may withdraw from the education component if they are unsuited to teaching, leaving the course with a BA or BSc. Courses include between 24 weeks and 32 weeks in the classroom and applications should be made via UCAS.

Postgraduate Certificate in Education (PGCE)
One-year full-time PGCE courses are for those who have already
completed a degree course appropriate to the subject they wish to
teach. There is a requirement that entrants to PGCE courses should
have at least 50 per cent of their post-GCSE education in National
Curriculum subjects. First degree courses should therefore be chosen
with care. Students with a first degree in National Curriculum
subjects will be in the strongest position but admissions tutors can
interpret other subjects favourably. A combined humanities degree,
for example, may still be considered adequate, especially if it is
backed up by A levels in National Curriculum subjects. The one-year
PGCE is currently the most popular route into secondary teaching
but there are also PGCE places for primary teaching. Apply via GTTR.

Two-year part-time PGCE
A limited number of courses, mainly in shortage subjects, including
mathematics, modern languages, business studies, design and
technology, the sciences, music and religious education are available.
Many of the students on these courses have family responsibilities or
other commitments which prevent them from attending a full-time
PGCE course. Courses are run subject to demand and applicants
should check with the relevant institution before naming them on
the Graduate Teacher Training Registry (GTTR) application form.

Two-year full-time subject conversion PGCE courses
Subject conversion courses are aimed at people who wish to teach
shortage subjects such as mathematics, science and modern foreign
languages. A conversion course is needed if you wish to teach a
subject that is not the subject of your first degree, for example
engineers wishing to teach mathematics. However, applicants must
still have completed at least a year of Higher Education study (at
degree or even HND level) directly relevant to the subject specialism.
Apply via the GTTR.

☐ OTHER ROUTES TO QUALIFIED TEACHER STATUS

The Open University (OU) part-time PGCE
A number of institutions offer a chance to obtain a PGCE through

part-time and distance learning study and they are listed in the GTTR handbook. The biggest provider in this mode however in the OU which has to be applied to directly. The OU offers a chance to obtain a PGCE through 18 months' part-time study combined with a number of full-time teaching placements. Courses begin in February of each year and are concluded in the following July. There are eight types of course on offer. Students choose between following a course for primary teaching with a chance to specialise in ages 5–8 or 7–11 or secondary subject courses in English, music, modern languages (French), history, mathematics, design and technology, and science.

The course confers QTS and is bound by the same regulations as other initial teacher training courses. However, it offers its students a very distinctive route into teaching.

The open learning approach of the OU is aimed primarily at mature students who, for reasons of geography or personal circumstance, need to combine full-time school experience with home-based study. Unusually for teacher training, over 80 per cent of the students on the course are aged over 30 and 75 per cent of the students are women, even in traditionally male-dominated subjects such as design and technology, and science. Many of these students are women returning to the job market after raising a family.

Students taking the course whilst working or coping with other commitments will find it requires a lot of self-discipline and even more motivation than usual. However, the OU stresses that its open learning is offered within a context of support from both the personal tutor assigned to the student by the university and by the mentor in the school where teaching practice takes place.

One of the advantages of the OU course is that students can spend their major work experience in a school nominated by themselves. Students often work in schools that they themselves attended as pupils and some work in schools which their children attend. The school, however, has to be chosen with care and will only be approved by the OU if it will provide the right range of teaching experience as well as suiting students' personal circumstances. The OU will advise on schools that have supported their students in the past, provide a letter of introduction to the school and negotiate with the school to ensure that it is appropriate and that it can provide an experienced teacher to act as a mentor to the student.

Students combining the course with a job will need to ensure they can attend three separate periods of full-time teaching experience including a six-week placement towards the end of the course. The course also includes four Saturday day schools which, as well as being an important academic part of the course, offer students a chance to reinforce contact with fellow students and exchange experiences.

The course materials make use of a variety of media including videos, audio tapes and set books. Students are loaned a personal computer, printer and modem to enable them to access the Internet and use electronic conferences to communicate with other students and their tutor. The course does not demand information technology (IT) skills from its students from the outset, even accepting non-word-processed essays in the early stages. However, most students quickly become familiar with the technology and move from nervousness about getting a PC out of its box to incorporating IT into their lesson planning. This kind of familiarity with IT can be a useful addition to a CV when it comes to applying for jobs. Apply directly to the OU. (Contact details are at the back of this book.)

Case study: A distance learning PGCE via the Open University
Newell Fisher is working as a prison officer but is completing a PGCE with the Open University and is hoping to work in secondary schools teaching English. Like many students on the OU course, Newell would have found it hard to have completed a full-time PGCE. 'I had a mortgage and could not have retrained for teaching through any other route,' says Newell. 'In fact, I considered other careers as well as teaching but none of them would have given me a chance to retrain without giving up my job.'

Newell initially considered a primary PGCE but found the course was full. 'In the end I am really glad I looked at secondary teaching,' says Newell. 'I think many students think teaching in secondary is like being a cop in New York but there are a lot of misconceptions about and it really isn't like that. From my point of view, I was attracted to secondary because I expect to teach a lot of drama and creative writing and that is more rewarding with older pupils. Also, while the cross-curricular nature of primary education did have its appeal, I also liked the challenge involved in being a subject specialist at secondary level.'

Before joining the Prison Service, Newell had taken a degree in drama and creative writing and he had kept up these interests.

This helped with his application and, he feels, will help make him a better teacher. 'I think I am an introverted extrovert,' says Newell. 'While I can seem a quiet, almost shy, person on a one-to-one basis, I can get on stage and perform to an audience and teaching does involve an element of performance.'

A feature of the OU course is that students have to locate a school that is willing to facilitate the periods of teaching practice and mentoring. 'I found that schools that had had previous contact with the OU course were quite interested, even if they weren't able to take me on, but other schools that didn't know about the OU course because, at that time at least, it was still relatively new, were much more wary,' says Newell. He has taken blocks of teaching practice in the school of three, four and six weeks. He has also taken a two-week block in a school nominated by the OU. 'I wasn't happy about the school they sent me to – a private girls' school but it was meant to be a contrasting experience. As it turned out, it was helpful from that point of view. Mind you, it wasn't as genteel as you might think.'

The teaching practice had to be fitted in with Newell's job. 'This was one of the most difficult aspects of the course,' says Newell. 'Organising my annual leave wasn't too bad, even though I had to take six weeks' unpaid leave and get a career development loan to cover my lost wages, but it does mean that I haven't had a proper holiday for two years and this can cause some strain, especially if you have a family. The important thing about this area is getting the support of your current employer. Employers need to be flexible about annual leave arrangements. I know some students have run into problems and one student got the sack over it.'

Another distinctive feature of the course is the use of information technology (IT). Like many of his fellow students, Newell was unused to computers but quickly adapted and finds it simply 'brilliant'. 'I have become a fairly confident user and use the computer and modem all the time to communicate with tutors and fellow students. I have what you could call a 'Campus on Computer' with conferences going on about my specialist subject, an international section and a social section. I am talking electronically to lots of people, most of whom I will never meet. The equipment the OU have loaned me is fine for electronic mail but a bit too slow for the Internet – for example, it took me three

*hours to download the works of Shakespeare. This is probably
a good thing, though, given that my phone bill has shot up
because I use it so much, more than is necessary really. Mind
you, their equipment is about to be upgraded.'*

*The IT and the 'top quality' supporting course material supplied by
the OU has helped overcome the isolation that could be a feature of
a distance learning course. Even so, Newell feels that more needs to
be done to support students. 'The OU provides a tutor but they are
there to mark your work and make sure you are up to standard.
They are not there to act in a counselling role and I think the OU is
aware that students might need that kind of support.'*

*Now that the course is coming to a conclusion Newell is looking
for a job in the state sector. 'Again, schools that have had
dealings with the OU course are interested but those that are not
familiar with it are less sure.' Newell is restricting his job hunt
to his own region which cuts down the number of schools he can
apply to but he still hopes to get work within a few months of the
course ending. 'Of course, the good thing about the way I have
done my training is that I am still doing a full-time job and so I
can afford to wait for the right job and school to come up. In the
meantime,' says Newell, 'I will be able to keep my hand in by
doing some occasional supply teaching.'*

School Centred Initial Teacher Training (SCITT)
SCITT is a one-year route for graduates to Qualified Teacher Status
(QTS) offering an alternative training route for those wishing to teach
in primary, secondary, sixth form and City Technology Colleges.
SCITT schemes are devised by consortia of local schools which
usually validate their course through Higher Education institutions,
enabling them to award a PGCE as well as the QTS. There are
currently over 30 SCITT schemes available and new schemes are
accepted regularly. The certificates they offer are equivalent to those
from Higher Education institutions and their students are just as
successful at getting jobs. However, because this is a relatively new
role and not, therefore, an automatic first choice for candidates,
SCITT schemes may be able to accommodate late applicants.

The majority of schemes are applied to through the GTTR but a
small number of schemes which choose not to be listed in the GTTR
can be contacted directly. The Teacher Training Agency provide the

authoritative list of schemes. SCITT courses carry a mandatory award. Students are also eligible for a flat-rate means-tested bursary for maintenance. In London the rate is £4,379 (secondary) and £4,527 (primary).

What is the SCITT experience?

As the name implies, School Centred Initial Teacher Training (SCITT) is a one-year route for graduates, offering students a high degree of exposure to schools during their training. The schemes are all individually approved by the Teacher Training Agency and they combine a classroom-based approach to training with an entitlement to individual counselling and the support of an appropriate mentor who is an experienced teacher in the school in which the student is based. The emphasis is on developing competence in classroom management and underpinning this with the progressive introduction to the theory behind the practice of teaching as the student gains confidence in his or her teaching skills.

Most of the course is spent in a base school but placements are arranged in other schools to offer a contrasting ethos and extend experience in the specialist subject on secondary courses, or to another key stage on primary courses.

Will I be thrown in the deep end?

Although by the end of your course you will be used to taking your own classes, you will spend much of the early part of the course observing and learning from an experienced teacher. Gradually, you will be introduced to teaching through 'team teaching', small group teaching, part-lesson teaching and then full-lesson teaching under the direct supervision of your mentor. The transition from observing to contributing through summing up or issuing instructions and eventually to taking your own classes is intended to build confidence. One student described how the process was so gradual that he only realised halfway through a class that 'Hey, I'm teaching on my own.' An independent survey in July 1995 rated classroom support as 'above average' or 'excellent'.

Will there be much reading and study?

Although SCITT courses are highly practical, there is a considerable study element. Courses combine theory with 'on-the- job' training and experience, encouraging students to be analytical, creative and reflective practitioners. All aspects of the course, including self-evaluation, completion of logs whilst on teaching practice and the completion of essays are assessed at the rigorous standard expected at postgraduate level. The course involves writing a number of essays covering topics such as how children learn, language and communication in the classroom, issues of gender and race and, for those on secondary courses, the role of your specialist subject in the National Curriculum. Essays are typically between 1500 and 3000 words and have to be fully referenced with bibliographies.

Case study: A PGCE in modern foreign languages via SCITT
Terry is completing a PGCE with the Chiltern Training Group, a consortium of Luton schools linked with the Open University and the University of Luton. This particular SCITT course is geared to preparing its students for work in the 11–18 range and, once he has completed it, Terry will be equipped to work with a secondary school, sixth form college or City Technology College.

Terry made a career change to teaching after having a successful career in the City of London as a manager in a human resources consultancy. 'Coming from recruitment I know it sounds like a cliché,' says Terry, 'but teaching was always something I wanted to do. Having just started a family it seemed like a perfect time to make a switch.'

Terry was able to decide on the SCITT training route relatively quickly. 'I had kept up my interest in education ever since I visited schools as a researcher into modern languages with Queen's University. I was familiar with the alternative routes into teaching and considered other options such as a traditional PGCE and the licensed teacher scheme but the SCITT route appealed to me because I really liked the idea of gaining the certificate from a base school and getting lots of on-the-job training with practising teachers.'

Terry felt she was accepted on the course partly because she had strong language skills. 'I had a French degree, had lived in and visited France regularly and even taught as an "assistante" there for a while. A second foreign language such as German or Spanish would have been helpful. 'My Gaelic is not in great demand in Luton,' says Terry, 'but I had acquired other skills in

*my career and had a strong commitment to teaching – after all,
I was giving up a well-paid job.'*

*The course has confirmed for Terry that she has made the right
choice of route. 'A SCITT course means your training takes place
in a base school with the support of a teacher who is a qualified
mentor. Even during the placement weeks, when you are
experiencing other types of schools, help is never very far away.'
The exposure to schools has brought other benefits too. 'I had
always kept in touch with French but the scheme meant I got
lots of opportunity to practise using and teaching it. I also got
lots of access to the resources of my school, including the school's
60 resident experts called teachers.'*

*As the course comes to a close Terry is applying for jobs. Many
students on SCITT schemes get jobs in the schools that make up
the consortium but there is no guarantee of employment. Terry is
offering English as a second subject but realises that many
schools now look for two foreign languages, even if the second
one is at a lower level. However, she is optimistic about finding
work. 'By the end of the course I will have already worked a full
school year, have taught GCSE classes on my own and will be
able to contribute quickly to a new school. 'However,' Terry adds,
'one of the drawbacks of the scheme, I suppose, is that I have
become so involved with my base school and have enjoyed my
time here so thoroughly that it will be a real wrench to have to
leave.'*

Licensed teaching

Licensed teachers are used by employers subject to local need with
limited places. Trainees on this route have to find a school to employ
them after which they are given a licence to teach for up to two years
when they can be recommended for Qualified Teacher Status. It is
generally a route for mature career changers who are 24 years or
above and often chosen by those who wish to obtain QTS but cannot
either get a grant or live on a grant. Graduates may be preferred
but, although it leads to QTS, it is not a PGCE route and those with
two years' successful experience of Higher Education – eg HND –
may be considered. Applicants also need to have attained and
demon-strated the standard equivalent to GCSE grade C in English
and mathematics. Vacancies may be advertised through Local
Education Authorities or with LEA-maintained schools, grant-

maintained schools and non-maintained special schools. The Licensed Teacher programme involves up to two years of practical training and study on-the-job. The licence to teach, which normally lasts up to two years, can be extended for part-time posts. Trainees who have at least two years' teaching experience teaching in, for instance, an independent school or an FE college may be eligible after a year. The governing body of the school at which you are employed has to design a suitable training programme which will consist of a variety of elements, for example training organised by the LEA or a Higher Education institution together with schools-based training provided by staff in the school or courses at a local college. Licensed teachers may be paid on the qualified teachers' scale or the unqualified teachers' scale as the governors consider appropriate.

In July 1993 there were 2,113 licensed teachers in primary and secondary schools in England and Wales (750 were overseas trained teachers, see below). There is currently little demand in the primary area. The Teacher Training Agency (TTA) may eventually act as a 'marriage bureau' between employers and applicants but currently there is no centralised list of employers offering this type of training and applicants should make informal approaches in their region. Training requirements are defined by the employer and the courses have not been inspected or their reputation fully established. However, the TTA has implemented strict quality control measures in order that the training standards on this scheme and on the Overseas Trained Teacher Scheme are comparable to those in other forms of initial teacher training.

The Graduate Teacher programme
The government has proposed from August 1997, an employment-based route into teaching, called the Graduate Teacher programme. The route can be seen as a variation on the Licensed Teacher scheme. However, if it goes ahead, it will only be open to those with degrees or equivalent and training will last from as little as one term to a maximum of one year. The minimum may be suitable for those who have worked as teachers overseas or in the independent sector. A new graduate with no professional training or relevant experience will be required to train for the maximum period. Responsibility for devising and delivering a training programme, and for recommending the award of QTS may be taken by the employing school or by other bodies, such as Teacher Training Institutes or even teacher supply

agencies, approved by the Teacher Training Agency.

Overseas teachers – authorisation to teach
This scheme is not aimed at qualified teachers from Scotland, Northern Ireland and other parts of the European Union. These may be granted QTS on application to the DfEE. Qualified teachers from the European Economic Area countries of Iceland and Norway are also eligible to apply for recognition. Information and forms (ask for form P5) are available from DfEE (Teacher Qualifications), Mowden Hall, Staindrop Road, Darlington DL3 9BG (tel: 01325 392123).

The Overseas Trained Teacher Scheme is aimed at teachers trained outside the European Economic Area wishing to obtain Qualified Teacher Status to enable them to teach in England and Wales. Applicants must have a degree in education, or a degree and a postgraduate teaching qualification and, in either case, one year's teaching experience. They must also have attained the standard equivalent to at least GCSE grade C in English language and mathematics. Applicants should contact the Local Education Authority where they wish to work, or respond to LEA or schools adverts making it clear that they do not hold QTS and wish to be employed as an overseas trained teacher. Suitably qualified overseas trained teachers may be employed immediately but have to undergo an induction programme before being recommended for QTS after a minimum of one term. Where possible, teachers from overseas could benefit from taking a longer route to QTS, such as a two-year BEd. This would offer a longer period of support in which to adjust to the different social background of teaching in the UK and to become aware of the different cultural contexts.

Further information on the Licensed Teacher and the Overseas Trained Teacher Schemes may be obtained from:

The Overseas Trained Teacher Administration Unit
Park Place Training
1 Princes Road
Ferndown
Dorset BH22 9JG
Tel: 01202 897691

Registered Teachers (for City Technology Colleges only)
To register for this scheme you have to be working as a prospective
Registered Teacher at a City Technology College and be
recommended for a training place to the Teacher Training Agency by
the college's governing body. The scheme is similar to the Licensed
Teacher scheme but run at even fewer institutions.

Training to teach in Further Education
Teachers in FE do not need a recognised qualification but completion
of a course will improve your chances of employment. You will
usually be required to have either a professional or academic
qualification in the subject you intend to teach and relevant
experience.

There are several awards which employers are increasingly
expecting candidates to offer. These include Higher Education
awards specifically designed to prepare students to teach in Further
Education. These are the:

One-year full-time PGCE (Further Education)
There are a number of courses specially designed for the FE sector
that are offered on a one-year full-time basis, or part-time for those
in service. The institutions are Bolton Institute, University of Wales
College of Cardiff, Keele University, University of Greenwich,
University of Huddersfield, University of Wales College Newport,
The Nottingham Trent University, University of Surrey, University
of Wolverhampton. The courses do not carry QTS and are not
suitable for those wishing to teach in schools. Courses are available
in subjects found in the FE sector such as accounting, beauty
therapy, languages, history and physics. Applications are made
direct to the institutions concerned but the GTTR *Guide for
Applicants* lists institutions and courses as does the *Handbook on
Initial Teacher Training in England and Wales* published by the
National Association of Teachers in Further and Higher Education
(NATFHE). Contact details for GTTR and NATFHE can be found at
the back of the book.

There are, however, some PGCE QTS courses which, because they
cover the 11–18 age range, may be able to offer teaching practice in a
post-16 or FE establishment. Institutions such as Edge Hill
University College, The University of Leicester and The University
of Wales, Swansea are examples of these. While the GTTR *Guide for
Applicants* has a full listing of PGCE Further Education courses not

all of them have to be applied to via the GTTR and applicants should apply direct to those institutions outside the GTTR system.

Certificate of Education (FE)
These are available as one-year full-time, or two-year part-time courses or through distance learning. The part-time option is usually taken by those already employed in a college. A degree is not necessarily needed for the CertEd but applicants should be able to offer maturity and a professional qualification in the subject they wish to teach. The University of Huddersfield offers a chance for those with the CertEd (FE) to go on to complete a BEd in Further Education.

Further information is available from the National Association of Teachers in Further and Higher Education (NATFHE) which produces a booklet on *Training to Teach in Further Education* and a *Handbook of Initial Teacher Training.*Contact details are at the back of this book.

City & Guilds
The City & Guilds' major national qualification for teachers is the Further and Adult Education Teachers' Certificate (City & Guilds 7306 or City & Guilds 7307 without NVQ accreditation). These part-time courses are designed for those already teaching adults or teaching in further education. The certificate does not lead to QTS and is at a lower level than the CertEd (FE). Many universities and colleges are now giving holders exemption from parts of the CertEd (FE).

RSA Examination Board
The RSA teachers' certificate and diploma courses are mainly in office studies, information technology and languages.

Case Study: A PGCE in further education
Gina is on the Postgraduate Certificate in Education course at Greenwich University. The course does not carry Qualified Teacher Status but prepares students for teaching post-compulsory education in Further Education colleges, sixth-form colleges, adult education centres and also in those independent schools that do not demand a QTS certificate.

Gina chose to go into teaching after a career in science in which she had worked for a number of years in the research department of London Zoo. 'It became increasingly difficult to get grants to do research. Also I had started a family and it was these things, together with the fact that I had had an enjoyable experience of teaching undergraduates that convinced me it was time for a change of direction towards teaching.'

Acceptance on the Greenwich course followed a rejection for an equivalent course at the London Institute of Education. 'I think the interviewer was very concerned that my research background and my experience of teaching undergraduates would mean that I wouldn't enjoy teaching basic science at the FE level. I was upset by the rejection but it did mean that I prepared much better for my application to Greenwich. I think they are very keen that you are clear why you are choosing FE rather than any other sector, such as secondary.'

Gina has found the course very practical with lots of opportunity to learn classroom technique. One of the units she had to pass towards the end of the course was a 'micro-teaching' unit culminating in teaching a class of fellow students and demonstrating a range of different teaching techniques – captured on video for help with later assessment. Even before completing the course, Gina has already undertaken 80 hours of teaching at a local FE college on a variety of courses – GCSE and A level biology, GNVQ Intermediate Science, Access courses for adults and, to her surprise, a class of 14 year olds from a local school taking a Steps Into Science course. 'One of the things admissions tutors – and employers – look for is a flexibility concerning the subjects you are prepared to teach,' says Gina. 'I hadn't had anything to do with A level biology for 20 years but the course will make you a trained teacher and you just have to use your study skills to get to grips with the subject matter. Also, I did not anticipate taking 14 year olds – especially those who are on courses at FE because they cannot cope with the level of courses at schools. One of the things that has become clear to me is that FE college lecturers have to deal with a wide variety of students.'

The practical experience of classroom teaching is given a theoretical background during the course of the year. Gina has had lectures on motivation, group work theory, equal opportunities, communication skills and assertiveness training. This last element, for example, is to help give trainee teachers the confidence to deal with groups of students. 'I think I already was a reasonably assertive person,' says Gina, 'but this unit was really about getting the balance right in a classroom situation.'

Other elements of the course are more directly geared to helping students get jobs. The potential changes flowing from the Dearing Report, for example, have been addressed by a unit on curriculum development which involved Gina in designing a new course that could be run at the local FE college. There has even been a unit on getting jobs, including lectures on filling out application forms. 'We became aware, during our time at the FE college,' said Gina, 'that the job market was getting more difficult. Ideally, I want to work in a sixth-form college but even though morale is low in FE I have enjoyed my experience of working in it.'

ROUTES TABLE

Name	Description	Length
Bachelor of Education (BEd)	full-time	3–4 years
Bachelor of Education (BEd)	full-time (shortage subjects)	2 years
Bachelor of Arts/Science with QTS (BA/BSc)	full-time	3–4 years
Postgraduate Certificate in Education (PGCE)	full-time/part-time	1–2 years
Postgraduate Certificate in Education – Further Education	full-time/part-time	1–2 years
Postgraduate Certificate in Education subject conversion	full-time	2 years
Postgraduate Certificate in Education Open University	distance learning part-time	18 months
School Centred Initial Teacher Training (SCITT)	full-time	1 year
Licensed Teaching	on-the-job training	2 years usually
Registered Teachers (for City Technology Colleges only)	on-the-job training	2 years usually
Overseas teacher scheme	on-the-job induction for those outside the EEA	at least 1 term
Graduate Teacher programme	on-the-job training	1 term to 1 year.

☐ WORK EXPERIENCE

Admissions tutors for initial teacher training (ITT) courses will need to be convinced that you are familiar with the culture of schools and have demonstrated some commitment to the career of teaching. They will understand that mature applicants with family responsibilities may not be able to spend as much time with a school as a younger graduate taking a year off after his or her degree, but getting some work experience in schools and with children is important before you start your course. It can be a condition for obtaining a place or gaining an interview. Leaving your first exposure to school until several months into your course may make it difficult to change your course if you decide the environment is not right for you. Ideally, you should aim to spend at least a day and ideally a week refreshing your memory about what schools are like and also noting how much they have changed.

It should not be too difficult to find a cooperative school to facilitate your visit, especially if the school is a reasonably large one. In fact, good schools are often keen to encourage interest in the teaching profession. You may offer your help with school trips, remedial reading or even the sports day. However, the most valuable experience for you will be to observe a variety of lessons – different subjects and age groups. You should also spend a substantial amount of time observing lessons in the subject you are planning to teach.

You will benefit most from your work experience if you are prepared. The class teacher will not have time to look after you during the class and you may well find yourself quickly becoming involved with the pupils. You may think you are 'just a visitor' but pupils may look on you as a resource to help them with their lessons. Be willing to help out and intervene where necessary. Above all, don't pester the teacher, especially during the class. At the end of your experience, you should have found out more about developments in the subject you may want to teach by having spoken to appropriate teachers. You should also have an idea about the impact of changes in education. Your application form should be informed by your personal experience.

Chapter Five
QUALIFICATIONS REQUIRED

Teaching has its own professional qualification, Qualified Teacher Status (QTS), which is obtained through taking a course of initial teacher training (ITT). Anyone wishing to teach in a maintained school needs this qualification. The only exceptions to this are those on schemes leading to QTS within a school or those working as 'instructors' (who will not be on permanent contracts). Having QTS, theoretically, enables you to work in either primary or secondary education but, realistically, you will need to take a conversion course if you want to switch between the two, since ITT courses generally encourage you to specialise.

Independent schools, Further Education colleges, sixth-form colleges and City Technology Colleges do not formally require applicants to have QTS but, increasingly, it is becoming difficult to get a job in these institutions without the professional qualification. Those wishing to teach in the post-16 sector may take the special courses designed for Further Education but should be aware that they do not necessarily confer QTS which will be needed to teach in a state school.

☐ ENTRY REQUIREMENTS

Teaching degrees

A minimum of five GCSEs (or the equivalent) at grade C or above, including English language and mathematics are needed for entry to teaching degrees. A broad range of GCSE subjects is encouraged for those entering all teaching courses.

Additionally, all entrants to initial teacher training primary courses after 1 September 1998 who were born after 1 September 1979 should also have attained GCSE grade C or above, in a single science subject or combined science. However, many Higher Education institutions are already looking for a science qualification. At some teacher training institutions mature applicants without the GCSE in science will be able to take an equivalence test in the same way that they can take tests in mathematics and English. At present, the science requirement does not apply to secondary courses but it may well be introduced eventually.

The GCSE requirements, particularly mathematics, can be a stumbling block for many applicants but they have been introduced because they are core education skills. The science GCSE has been brought in for primary courses because teachers in that sector have to teach the broad range of subjects covered by the National Curriculum and this includes science.

However, institutions can exercise discretion and those without the core qualifications should contact them directly.

Equivalent qualifications are accepted. Typically these include CSE grade 1 or appropriate BTEC National/GNVQ modules. BTEC National equivalents to GCSE mathematics are Numerical Methods and Finance. GCSE English equivalents include BTEC modules in Communication Skills, and People and Organisations. Applicants offering GNVQ Intermediate level qualifications, however, may find that institutions do not accept their mathematics and English content to be equivalent to GCSE.

Many colleges offer equivalence tests in English and mathematics for those without the appropriate qualifications and some are offering similar tests for science. Mature students without GCSEs who offer degree or Access courses that have covered core subjects may find that institutions consider these to be acceptable. A supporting statement from an Access course tutor testifying to the level of mathematics on the course may even avoid the need for students to take an equivalence test. Equivalence tests taken at one institution are not transferable to other ITT institutions. Candidates usually need to have the required GCSE qualifications at the time of application but some institutions will accept students on a provisional basis if they have made arrangements to obtain the GCSEs before the teacher training course begins.

Overseas teachers will need transcripts of their certificates.

A levels and teaching
You do not necessarily need A levels to obtain a place on a teacher

training course since other equivalent level qualifications can be accepted (eg BTEC National, GNVQ Advanced, Access course). However, if you are applying with A levels you must have at least one A level, and preferably more, in subjects appropriate to the primary or secondary curriculum. AS qualifications are accepted as half of A levels. The National Curriculum subjects are divided into core – English, mathematics, science – and foundation subjects – art, geography, history, modern foreign languages (11-16 years only), music, physical education and technology (including design). Religious education is not part of the National Curriculum but is required to be taught by law.

Trainee primary teachers learn to teach all the primary curriculum subjects but may specialise in one or more subjects. Secondary teachers can train to teach National Curriculum subjects and also subjects that are part of the broader curriculum – for example business studies, economics, sociology. Secondary teachers may teach two or more distinct subjects.

BTEC National/GNVQ Advanced and teaching
Although GNVQ Advanced level and BTEC National courses are equivalent to two A levels, the content of some courses is not often relevant to the National Curriculum. In these cases a well-balanced package of qualifications is important for entry into teaching, including a good set of GCSEs and sometimes an additional A level. Candidates should use the personal statement to draw out the relevance of their vocational course to teaching. Any additional extension units or A level taken should also be included. As noted earlier, GNVQ Intermediate qualifications are not considered to meet the mathematics and English GCSE requirements.

Admissions tutors pay great attention to course content. Even students with straight grade As at A level can encounter problems if the subject matter is inappropriate. Some vocational courses, however, do have a National Curriculum basis in science, mathematics or art and applicants with merits and distinctions will be able to apply with confidence.

Other courses such as hotel and catering, health and social care or leisure and tourism have no National Curriculum subject base and applicants with these qualifications may find it harder to be accepted on to some courses. Such applicants are sometimes accepted on to early years of general degrees with Qualified Teacher Status and on to some physical education and biology courses. Students considering taking courses in these and other vocational areas would be well advised to take additional units or an A level alongside their course. It would also be worth their while to contact Higher Education institutions before embarking on their GNVQ or BTEC National course to check out what additional courses they will need in order to be able to apply for an ITT course. A higher success rate has been achieved where there are close partnerships between schools, FE colleges and local Higher Education institutions. Students embarking on a GNVQ Advanced course should consider taking optional modules that are as relevant as possible to the National Curriculum, if they eventually wish to take an initial teacher training course.

Some institutions have indicated that a combination of GNVQ and a relevant A level will be required. However, good GNVQ students will still be able to apply to some courses without this additional qualification.

Contact teacher training admissions tutors for advice as each institution decides if an applicant's qualifications meet the appropriate criteria.

Access routes to teaching
Some Access courses are recognised as meeting the entry requirements for degree courses with Qualified Teacher Status but applicants should check their acceptability with the institutions offering the teacher training courses that interest them. Courses with mathematics, English and science components are likely to achieve a more favourable response. Some institutions automatically offer places on initial teacher training courses to students who pass the Access courses.

Appropriate degrees for PGCE
Candidates for PGCE training, whether for primary, secondary or further education teaching, need to hold a degree, or degree equivalent qualification, appropriate to the curriculum subject they wish to teach. Institutions decide if an applicant's qualifications meet these criteria. Those offering degrees from overseas will have their degrees checked against the British Council approved list. It is important that candidates ensure that this check is carried out as

soon as possible, and before submitting their application to the Graduate Teacher Training Registry, to avoid disappointment, especially as some overseas degrees are not considered to be equivalent. Students with qualifications from India and Pakistan, for example, will need to offer an MA .

Appropriate degrees for primary and secondary teaching
Formally, institutions need to 'satisfy themselves that the content of postgraduate students' first degrees provides the necessary foundation for work as a primary school teacher'. Those with degrees in subjects such as sociology, law, philosophy and modern languages may have more difficulty in obtaining a primary teaching place. However, they can still be considered if they can show that at least 50 per cent of their post-GCSE education has been in subjects related to the National Curriculum. The main concern of admissions tutors is to accept students who will make good primary teachers. However, given the competition for places on primary courses, many will feel obliged to favour those whose qualifications are most directly relevant.

Applicants will need to take care to relate their previous post-compulsory education to the curriculum, especially if their degree is not clearly relevant. For example, an applicant with a degree in Caribbean Studies might note on the application form that 20 per cent of the course was devoted to literature with one module on Black British writers and a 3,000-word dissertation on 'Shakespeare and race - The Tempest and Othello', and that 20 per cent was devoted to history with one module on Africans and native Americans and a 3,000-word dissertation on Afro-Caribbeans in the Great War! Admissions tutors may be able to offer further advice.

Secondary applicants will need to demonstrate that their degree courses are relevant to the subject they wish to teach. Those whose degree titles do not obviously relate to the National Curriculum will need to give a breakdown of their degree course content. While institutions are at liberty to interpret the content of previous education, most are insisting that at least 50 per cent of an applicant's post-compulsory education must be relevant. The only possible exceptions to this might be religious education, physical education or modern foreign languages for native-speaking foreign national graduates. The rise of the modular degree has made it more difficult for admissions tutors to assess how relevant certain degree courses are. It is recommended that those with degree courses with titles such as Combined Studies should be quite explicit in highlighting the relevance of their courses. One admissions tutor on a PGCE English course, for example, suggests that applicants write 'contains literature' against modules such as Caribbean Studies or Classics or any other where the literature content may not be obvious. It is also the case that even those applicants with a directly relevant degree such as mathematics will still need to be able to discuss the relevance of their degree to the National Curriculum. After all, the content of mathematics degree courses is quite different from the mathematics a primary school teacher will be teaching.

It is not true that postgraduate students always need a degree in a National Curriculum subject. Subjects such as politics, law and philosophy, while less acceptable, can have a case made for their relevance. However, it may be more difficult for students with leisure and tourism degrees wishing to teach English or History, for example, to convince admissions tutors that their degrees contain an adequate percentage of National Curriculum material. Psychology degrees and other less explicitly relevant degrees are accepted by some universities, such as Leicester and Nottingham Trent. Leicester accepts psychology degrees for its Primary course because it leads on to a course in Educational Psychology for Psychology graduates wishing to gain teaching experience prior to possible training as Educational Psychologists. Such institutions will pay particular attention to candidates' other academic qualifications, such as A levels as well as other qualities applicants may bring. If in doubt, consult the institutions' admission tutors before submitting an application.

A note for those with Higher National Diploma (HND) qualifications. Entrants to PGCE courses must have a degree. However, there are a number of routes into teaching for Diplomates including the two-year BEd in shortage secondary subjects (through UCAS) and the licensed teachers scheme. Alternatively, students may transfer on to a relevant three-year degree course and then take a PGCE or transfer on to a four-year BEd course. HND students applying for a BEd would very probably not be offered any exemptions despite their previous Higher Education experience and would have to be prepared to take the course from the beginning. However, the introduction of GNVQs to schools and the fact that the curriculum now includes a significant percentage of time (20 per cent) devoted to vocational subjects means there could be an increasing demand for students with an HND background.

Chapter Six
THE APPLICATION PROCESS

Teaching is a popular career choice. While some courses receive a shortfall of applications many other teacher training courses are heavily oversubscribed. One institution, for example, offering a BEd primary course received 1500 applications for 117 places. This made it more difficult to get into than the University of Cambridge! Another institution offering PGCE courses currently has 143 students only four of whom have a third-class degree. Of its teacher training students, 60 per cent have either a 2:1 or 2:2 first degree. In 1995, 33,830 applications were processed for PGCE courses, a four per cent increase on 1994.

Your chances of a successful application may be affected by the fact that some courses are quite small or some institutions are particularly popular. Admissions tutors for primary schemes are keen to receive applications from those with qualifications in science, mathematics and technology. Competition for a PGCE place is tough for primary and also secondary biology, history, English and geography. The Survey of Selection Criteria and Procedures booklets produced by AGCAS (Association of Graduate Careers Advisory Services) can give you further information about the competition for places. Certainly some courses, such as those covered by the Priority Subject Recruitment Scheme, may be less competitive. Applications for PGCE mathematics courses fell by 14 per cent in 1996 and those for physics fell by 25 per cent. Despite this, the focus of admissions tutors always remains steady: to select only those candidates who will not just cope with the demanding courses but go on to make good teachers. Stringent entry standards are being maintained, particularly as initial teacher training institutions are to be partly allocated places based on the number of their students successfully obtaining jobs after the course.

The application form for teacher training is especially important because entry procedures for courses demand that admissions tutors interview all candidates who are accepted. This involves an unusual amount of interviewing by colleges and application forms have to make the strongest possible case for you to persuade tutors that you warrant an interview. There are a number of issues that applicants will need to be aware of. (Applicants should also read *Applying For Teacher Training*, published by AGCAS.)

☐ APPLYING FOR BED AND BSC/BA COURSES

Applying for Degree Courses for Teaching Training
Those wishing to gain Qualified Teacher Training Status as part of a degree course (BA/BSC with QTS or BEd) must apply through the University Central Admissions System (UCAS). The official reference book is *University and College Entrance: The Official Guide* which contains a section on Teacher Training courses and UCAS also publishes *The UCAS Handbook* which gives a detailed list of universities and colleges and the courses they offer. Applicants should also take care to read the prospectuses published by individual institutions and make sure they are going to have the necessary entrance qualifications before the course begins. UCAS has a Web site at http://www.ucas.ac.uk/

The Handbook and application forms are available directly from UCAS if you do not have access via your school or college. Write to: UCAS, Fulton House, Jessop Avenue, Cheltenham, Gloucestershire, GL50 3SH.

You can enter up to six choices of courses at university/college and the entrance fee for 1998 entry is £12. You may apply for a single course at one institution only for a reduced fee but, given the generally popular nature of teaching degrees, applicants are recommended to apply to the maximum number of courses.

The normal deadline for applications to reach UCAS is December 15th in the year before entry but you are urged to apply as early as possible once you have made your mind up about your choices. Late applicants are considered at the discretion of individual institutions.

Clearing is a special service operated by UCAS in July/August/September for those still seeking a place, and for late applicants applying after 30 June.

☐ APPLYING FOR PGCE COURSES

The Graduate Teacher Training Registry (GTTR) fields applications for places on the majority of courses. The application fee for 1998 entry is £10. Contact details for GTTR are in the further information section at the back of this book. However, those wishing to train to teach in Scotland or Northern Ireland should contact:

Scotland
Advisory Service on Entry to Teaching, 5 Royal Terrace, Edinburgh EH7 5AF
Teacher Education Admission Clearing House (TEACH), PO Box 165, Edinburgh EH8 8AT

Northern Ireland
Northern Ireland Education Office, Rathgael House, Balloo Road, Bangor, County Down BT19 2PR (tel: 01247 270077).

The GTTR provides a free *Guide for Applicants* published in September of each year which includes a full list of courses and procedures and the application form. This guide can be used in conjunction with course prospectuses, the course surveys published by AGCAS, the *Handbook of Initial Teacher Training* and the publication *Applying For Teacher Training*, also published by AGCAS.

The PGCE application timetable
Application forms are available from the Graduate Teacher Training Registry from 1 September. While there is no closing date for applications it is advisable to apply as early as possible as popular courses and subjects can fill up quickly, sometimes by as early as October. More importantly, however, apply only when you are sure you are going to be able to submit the best application you can and you have been able to research which institutions you want to apply for. In any case the GTTR does not submit the first batch of applications to colleges until around October of each year and then sends out batches weekly right up until the beginning of courses in the following academic year. If you have not been placed by June or July of the year in which you wish to start your training you may need to review your interest in, and suitability for, teaching. Many students obtain places quite late and the GTTR runs an unplaced

student scheme around August of the year of entry which gives you another chance of obtaining an interview by circulating your details again. Applicants cannot apply directly to individual institutions but may contact them towards the end of August to check if they have any last-minute vacancies through other students withdrawing, for example. All applications must be made through the GTTR.

Academic background

The previous chapter (Qualifications Required) gives more detail about the specific academic qualifications required but candidates should be aware that teacher training courses in general demand a high academic standard. The Post Graduate Certificate in Education, for example, is precisely that: postgraduate. Those teaching at the primary level are said to require an almost Renaissance breadth of knowledge to be able to teach the ten subjects demanded by the National Curriculum. Good academic ability is a key requirement. Those applying for PGCE courses with third-class degrees, for example, will need to convince admissions tutors that they can cope with the intellectual demands of the course.

Aptitude

Even those who are acceptable academically need also to be the kind of person who will eventually make a good teacher. Admissions tutors have to make professional judgements very early on about an applicant's aptitude for a teaching career. This is why they are obliged to interview all the students they accept on teacher training courses. It is also why the application form is a crucial first stage in the procedure.

The application form

Colleges have a legal obligation to interview all students before they are accepted on to ITT courses. This means there is less time to interview borderline candidates and makes it even more important to submit a strong application. Nevertheless, admissions tutors are surprised at how many poorly completed application forms they receive. Pay attention to each of the following:

- *Presentation*
  Teachers have to communicate to pupils through the blackboard, for example, and a scruffy application form does not inspire confidence that you would be able to do that well.

68

- ***Language***
  Use standard written English throughout. This is the medium used by teachers for communicating in reports, in presenting curriculum policy and in letters to parents, for example. Use of non-standard English on the course for essays and in exams would, in any case, mean failing the course. Correct spelling and the correct use of upper and low case are essential. Application forms with poor spelling and with statements 'Shouting' through the over use of upper case will automatically be rejected, regardless of their content. Young pupils especially can have problems using upper and lower case properly and teacher training courses simply do not have the time to teach students these basics.

- ***Use all available space***
  While it is unnecessary to include extra supporting material, you should make full use of the space allotted on the form for the additional information.

- ***Evidence of work or involvement with young people***
  Admissions tutors to ITT courses will need to be convinced that you know what schools are like. It is important to gain work experience in schools and with children before you start your course and the completion of work experience can be a condition for gaining an interview or obtaining a place. You should aim to spend at least a day and preferably a week refreshing your memory about what schools are like and also noting how much they have changed. See the section on work experience at the end of Chapter 4 for further advice.

- ***Reasons for wanting to teach***
  Those who want to teach because they 'love children' may find it difficult to persuade admissions tutors that they could cope with the range of children they will be responsible for including, it has to be acknowledged, some apparently 'unlovely' children.

- ***Current education issues***
  You will certainly be asked to demonstrate your understanding of the breadth and content of the National Curriculum in an interview and those applying for postgraduate courses should be able to relate their degree subject knowledge to the National Curriculum. Applicants should be clear what they would be teaching and at what

age. Copies of the National Curriculum are available from The Stationery Office or on the Internet (see Chapter 3).

- ***Equal opportunities***
  You should demonstrate an understanding of the importance of equal opportunities issues.

☐ HEALTH AND FITNESS

All applicants have to complete a self-declaration health form and some may be required to submit to, and pay for, a formal medical examination. It is unwise to disguise any problems you may have had. Those susceptible to breakdowns or those with drink problems or those who needed to take Valium to get through exams should consider whether they can cope with the stress of a teaching career.

☐ CRIMINAL CONVICTIONS

It is a requirement of the Rehabilitation of Offenders Act (1974) that all those seeking entry to the teaching profession disclose any criminal convictions or pending proceedings against them. A police check will be made before you are employed by a school. Prospective applicants have to make written consent to a police check being made before they can be employed by a school. A criminal conviction will not automatically prevent you from becoming a teacher. Local Education Authorities and many individual schools have their own policy with regard to criminal conviction.

☐ TEACHING TRAINING AND DISABILITY

The Department for Education and Employment regulations stress that training colleges must satisfy themselves that candidates are medically fit for the course and for subsequent employment as a teacher. The most recent guidance (Circular 13/93) contains positive statements on disabled candidates, particularly that 'Disability in itself does not mean that a teacher is medically unfit. Disabled teachers can contribute to the overall school curriculum in terms of raising the aspirations of disabled pupils and educate non-disabled people about the reality of having a disability.' The Circular goes on to state that neither a severe hearing loss nor visual impairment is in itself a bar to teaching. Despite these encouraging statements applicants with disabilities need to be prepared for a rough ride. Only about 0.1 per cent of teachers are registered as disabled and applicants will need to plan their application carefully to overcome difficulties and pursue their chosen career. You may contact the DfEE for information about entry into teaching for disabled people on 0171 925 6020.

Choosing your route into teaching

Applicants will need to decide which route will work best for them. Some may obtain a non-teaching degree before applying for a PGCE because this gives them the security of a degree in case teacher training does not suit them. A number of BA and BSc courses developed recently that also award QTS may be of interest to these candidates. Others may consider that a BEd and its longer periods of teaching practice may be the best way to prove their ability to teach.

Whichever route is preferred it is strongly recommended that applicants visit likely training institutions to check that the college will suit them and to establish what support will be available on teaching practice. Colleges sometimes turn down disabled applicants because they are unable to find a school that is either suitable or willing to accommodate the student on teaching practice. One possible solution in this situation is to consider the Open University PGCE route which allows students to organise their own teaching practice school.

'Fitness to Teach'

Colleges must establish that applicants meet the statutory requirement partly through the institution's medical adviser's assessment of the candidates' 'Declaration of Health'. They may also require a candidate to undertake a medical examination. Eventually the medical adviser will make a recommendation and this heavily influences the decision of the college on admission. If you disagree with the recommendation you may still employ arguments to persuade the college in your favour, for example, by citing previous experience in a school or similar setting, by suggesting that a practising disabled teacher assist in the interview and selection procedure.

Funding

There are a number of additional grants available for those with disabilities. These include:

- a grant to cover the costs of non-medical personal support for extra tuition, note-takers or interpreters, for example

- a grant for equipment such as a PC or adapted computer, a scanner or radio aid

- other funding for photocopying costs, extra books and extra travel costs.

Getting a job

The same regulations govern employment as cover entry to teacher training but by this stage you will have the advantage of having demonstrated one of the most important qualities a teacher may need – dedication. You may also be able to offer the employer's medical examiner letters of recommendation from your course director or from the school where you did your teaching practice. The booklet published by the Royal Association for Disability and Rehabilitation (RADAR) entitled *So You Want to Be a Teacher?* gives a lot of information and guidance for disabled applicants. You will find the address of RADAR at the back of the book.

Chapter Seven
INTERVIEWS

Because teaching depends so much on the ability of teachers to communicate well, the interview is an integral part of the admissions procedure. Even students applying from abroad can expect to have to attend an interview. Applicants need to be able to convince the interviewer that they will be able to stand in front of a class of pupils and have enough 'presence' to command their attention and respect. Those who find it difficult to make eye contact or whose voice is naturally very quiet may need to make a conscious effort to change these aspects of themselves. There are a number of important areas that Admissions Tutors will look for evidence of in the interview:

- commitment to work with pupils of all levels of ability
- evidence of work with children
- a realistic attitude towards children and teaching
- ideas about how to plan a lesson
- knowledge of current issues in education/developments in school
- a realistic but positive view of schools and schooling.

☐ PERSONAL QUALITIES

Interviewers will look for evidence of a candidate's:

- ability to express him or herself clearly and logically in conversation in English
- capacity to reflect on his or her own educational experience
- sense of responsibility and commitment to teaching
- ability to listen and be sensitive to others
- potential to relate well with children
- enthusiasm and energy
- sense of humour
- stamina and robustness;
- smart appearance, maturity and clarity of speech
- competence in learning and an ability to learn fast.

☐ TYPICAL INTERVIEW QUESTIONS

These might include:

- Why do you want to teach?
- What do you know about the National Curriculum?
- How would you deal with an aggressive parent?
- Should pupils have to take exams?
- What makes a good mathematics teacher? (mathematics subject applicant)
- How would you motivate an uninterested pupil?
- How relevant is your degree to teaching your chosen subject (secondary)?
- How could your outside interests be used in the classroom?
- How would you interest a Year 9 pupil in Shakespeare? (English subject applicant)

Interviews can take different forms. The interview may consist of a panel and include someone from a local school as well as someone from the ITT institution. Applicants may be interviewed in small groups or even quite large groups of up to 15 in which you are asked to discuss education issues. Sometimes you may be asked to do something practical such as plan and present a lesson or stand at the back of the room and 'project' your voice or even enter the interview room pretending it is a class of noisy pupils.

Further information can be obtained from the publication *Applying For Teacher Training* published by AGCAS.

There is extra funding available for those training in shortage subjects in England, Wales and Northern Ireland. In England the Priority Subject Recruitment Scheme grant from the Teacher Training Agency can offer awards in the following subject areas:

- mathematics
- information technology
- design and technology
- science (physics, chemistry, biology)
- modern foreign languages
- Welsh (in Wales)
- religious education.

In England the awards are distributed through teaching institutions which have had to apply to the Teacher Training Agency. Not all institutions will have been awarded or even have applied for these funds and you may wish to check the situation with the TTA before choosing your course. For courses in Wales contact the Higher Education Funding Council for Wales, telephone 01222 682224. For Northern Ireland contact the individual teacher training institutions. There are no shortage subject bursaries in Scotland, or for those taking a PGCE (FE) or for the Open University PGCE. The amount of grants will vary from institution to institution. Brunel University, for example, awards £1000 for science students with at least a 2:2 degree and also scholarships of £1000 to students from ethnic minorities. The University of the West of England at Bristol awards up to £750 on its two-year BA/BSc QTS course for those with dependent children and an extra £250 if students have merit or distinction HND. Other courses offer funding in the form of help with child care. The publication *Initial Teacher Training Shortage Subject Bursaries* published by the University of Manchester and UMIST Careers Service offers a reasonably comprehensive list of current award holding courses – see Further Information on page 00.

Chapter Nine
TEACHING SALARIES

A recent survey conducted on behalf on the Teacher Training Agency found that teaching is perceived to be a poorly rewarded career financially. Of respondents surveyed, 18 per cent believed that newly qualified teachers earned less than £10,000 and 49 per cent believed they earned between £10,000 and £15,000. In fact, since December 1996 honours graduates in their first year of teaching started on at least £14,001, around the average for graduates. Some schools may pay more to encourage applicants or to recognise pre-teaching work experience.

Here are some comparisons:

Average weekly pay £	Male	Female
Social worker/probation officer	354.50	333.60
Author/writer/journalist	380.00	398.50
Secondary school teacher*	463.80	407.80
Solicitor	664.40	488.20
Chartered accountant	508.90	432.20

* (includes head teacher)

Teaching unions are concerned that pay deals for teachers should encourage more applicants to teacher training courses. Teachers in primary and secondary education are paid on a common pay scale which starts at £14,001 on point 2 rising to £33,375 on point 17. Additional allowances are paid for those teaching in and around London. Each year teachers move up one point on the scale with the possibility of extra half-point rises to recognise excellent teaching or extra responsibility. Progress to point 10, and a salary of £22,194 currently, is automatic. After this, progress is dependent on taking on extra responsibility such as Special Education Needs Co-ordinator or subject co-ordinator (this may be more possible in the larger schools common to the secondary sector).

Chapter Ten
WHAT LIES AHEAD?

In May 1997 the Labour Party was elected after a campaign that had 'education, education, education' written on its masthead. Once in power it took commentators and education professionals aback with the speed with which it moved to implement its policies on education.

The theme of its approach as stated by the new Education and Employment Secretary is to concentrate on 'standards, standards, standards.' Two Education Bills feature at the top of the Government's agenda. These will:

• Reduce primary school class sizes for five, six and seven year olds to 30 and under by using money freed up by the abolition of the Assisted Places Scheme.

• Introduce tough new national targets on numeracy and literacy. 1996 figures showed that only 55% of 11 year olds reached the standard in maths expected for their age and in English tests only 57% could read at the same standard. By the time of national tests in 2002, David Blunkett announced, 75% of 11 years olds will be reaching the standards expected for their age in maths and 80% will be reaching the standards expected in English. A new Standards and Effectiveness Unit was also set up within the DfEE to drive forward Government policy on raising standards in all schools and to help meet the targets for primary literacy and numeracy. The Unit will also oversee the work of the Literacy Task Force that has been joined by a newly created Numeracy Task Force which will also help deliver these targets. The introduction of these targets will raise questions about the nature and range of the primary curriculum. Some educationalists claim that will only be delivered by cutting down the number of subjects featured in the primary curriculum.

The drive on standards combines support and pressure. A Special Measure Action Recovery Team (SMART) will offer failing schools the chance to utilise the skills of a team of experts. Schools which continue to fail will be closed down. Additionally failure in schools will be rooted out by the introduction of new procedures for 'dealing swiftly with failing teachers'.

- Introduce a new framework of foundation, community and aided schools which will incorporate the grant-maintained sector. Community schools will broadly equate with previous local authority schools while foundation and aided schools will own their assets. Meanwhile schools will still be allowed to apply for, and be given, Grant-maintained status

- Improve the vocational and preparation of children by developing the curriculum for 14-19 year olds and providing work experience for 14-16 year olds. These measures will raise the profile of vocational qualifications in schools.

- Establish a General Teaching Council which will be responsible for regulating the teaching profession and promoting teaching as a career.

The plans for a teacher training national curriculum due to be implemented in September 1997 are being reviewed by David Blunkett. Labour will not scrap the plans, developed by The Teacher Training Agency, but will reconsider the detail.

The government's plans to provide employment and training for 250,000 unemployed young people, funded by the windfall tax, is expected to increase the number of students at further education colleges.

Chapter Eleven
LECTURING IN HIGHER EDUCATION

Higher Education has grown dramatically in the UK. Student numbers have risen from 25,000 at 25 universities in 1962 to a million students at over 100 institutions in 1996. New entrants to the lecturing profession rose from 1,486 in 1989 to 1,686 in 1993. This growth in numbers has been driven partly by the fact that large numbers of academics are reaching retirement age. According to 1993 figures, nine universities have 20 per cent or more staff aged over 55. Some institutions now operate an early retirement programme for lecturers from the age of 50. Older staff are more expensive than their juniors and there is an incentive amongst university managers to let senior academics go.

However, the increase in staff numbers has been more than outweighed by the rising numbers of students. The National Postgraduate Committee which represents doctoral students says that its members are finding it harder than ever to find a first teaching post. Many institutions are expecting to make staff redundancies and increase the numbers of staff employed on a part-time or temporary basis. The increase in initiatives such as the introduction of top-up fees is unlikely to reverse this trend.

Those seeking posts will need a very good honours degree together with higher degrees such as a PhD in a relevant field together with a proven research record and, most importantly, a list of publications to their name.

Lecturers are expected to conduct original research as well as teach increasing numbers of students and there can sometimes be a conflict between these demands. Typically, lecturers will be responsible for teaching large groups of students and taking smaller tutorial sessions as well as supervising, advising and examining students in their specialist area. The research often involves managing and budgeting a research group, writing research proposals and gaining funding.

Traditionally, there has been little emphasis on formal teaching certificates as entry qualifications. Some PGCEs that prepare students for work in the FE sector also include an orientation to Higher Education but this is by no means the main route into the profession.

Most postgraduate students expect to teach in order to earn their way through their studies. This provides good experience and a basis for making contacts with other academics. While vacancies are advertised in the *Times Higher Education Supplement* and the *Guardian* on Tuesday, this kind of networking and the personal recommendations that may flow from them enhance your chances of success.

Many institutions have graduate teaching assistant (GTA) posts which typically involve a third of a teaching load for a third of a lecturer's salary plus PhD tuition and examination fees. The use of postgraduate students for teaching has been a feature at the universities of Oxford and Cambridge for many years but is now part of the strategic plans of other universities.

GTA programmes include training in basic classroom techniques to enable courses to be delivered to a basic standard of competence. It is less common for programmes to cover selecting course content, course design and evaluation. Those who successfully make the transition to a salaried post may be encouraged to obtain an in-service teaching qualification such as the Certificate in Teaching in Higher Education.

Chapter Twelve
TEACHING ENGLISH AS A FOREIGN LANGUAGE

Teaching English as a foreign language (TEFL) is an excellent way to travel, see new countries and to meet people from different cultures. English is the language of international communications and there is worldwide demand for teachers of English with opportunities to teach in Europe, South America and Asia. However, there is also a well-established network of language schools and colleges in the UK and it is possible for suitably qualified teachers to pursue a long-term career in this country. However, competition for a limited number of positions in the UK can be fierce. Those who continue tend to gain two or three years' experience and then do higher level Diploma TEFL courses. It is then possible to train to become a trainer of TEFL teachers, go into management or write TEFL books and resources.

Many of those who go into TEFL work do so as a temporary measure. Two-thirds of people who complete a RSA TEFL course, for example, just do two or three years of TEFL and then go into another career. However, those who wish to work in the industry will find a buoyant demand both overseas and, mainly in the summer for short courses, in the UK.

You can get some jobs without a TEFL qualification but this is becoming more difficult and the pay and work conditions are generally worse than for those jobs requiring a qualification. For those considering TEFL some of the pros and cons are:

Pros
•Travel
•People-based work
•Opportunity to learn new languages
•Seeing and integrating into new cultures
•Interesting work
•Career opportunities (some)

Cons
•Money
•Lack of tempting career structure
•Difficulties of adjustment on return to UK

☐ THE QUALIFICATIONS AVAILABLE

There are a number of ways to become a teacher of English as a foreign language but confusion can arise because of the variety of routes and the acronyms they involve. The most widely recognised areas of work and qualifications are as follows:

TEFL (Teaching English as a Foreign Language)/TESOL (Teaching English to Speakers of Other Languages).
These mean the same thing. Teaching is directed to non-native speakers in private language schools in the UK and overseas and in UK state colleges. Students may be learning for leisure purposes, to pass exams, to get into an English-speaking university or for a job.

TESL (Teaching English as a Second Language)
Sometimes called ESL, TESL opportunities are found in the UK and overseas but they have their own specific objectives. However, there are overlaps with TEFL/TESOL and teachers often move from one to the other. In the UK, TESL involves teaching individuals from ethnic minority groups who need to acquire an adequate knowledge of the language to help them integrate into British education, employment and culture. Overseas TESL is typically used in countries such as Nigeria and Singapore where English is the language of administration and communication between different language groups. More information on TESL may be obtained by contacting the National Association for Teaching English and other Community Languages to Adults. See the Useful Addresses section at the end of this chapter.

English for Specific Purposes (ESP)
There is a growing demand from students who wish to learn English with particular application to vocational areas such as business, medicine or engineering. Teachers in this sector will have to acquire some knowledge of the specific area and become familiar with correct terminology but there is a lot of general language work involved as well.

☐ TRAINING

The most widely recognised and available qualification is the Certificate in the Teaching of English as a Foreign Language to Adults (CTEFLA). In October 1996, this was redesignated the Certificate in English Language Teaching to Adults (CELTA). It is offered by the Royal Society of Arts Examination Board/University of Cambridge Local Examinations Syndicate (RSA Cambridge). A similar qualification, the Certificate in Teaching of English to Speakers of Other Languages (TESOL), is offered by Trinity College London. Both courses combine theory and practice and take around four weeks full-time, although part-time options are also available. Courses can cost between £700 and £1000 and are intensive and demanding. While these courses are introductory they do prepare participants for their first job. The addresses for RSA and Trinity College can be found at the end of this chapter. A list of introductory courses can also be found in *The ELT Guide: The definitive guide to Teaching English as a Foreign Language.*

After taking the introductory courses and gaining around two to three years' teaching experience it is possible to take Diploma level courses. The RSA Cambridge Diploma in Teaching English as a Foreign Language to Adults (DTEFLA) is offered mainly part-time as an 'in-service' qualification. It can be useful for those wishing to move into teaching in further education or in private language schools or for those intending to take up posts overseas. Trinity College offers an advanced Licentiate Diploma for Teachers of English to Speakers of Other Languages. Candidates are strongly advised to follow a course at a registered centre or enrol on a distance learning course before sitting the exams, although this is not a formal requirement. The RSA Cambridge Diploma in Teaching English as a Foreign Language to Adults (DTEFLA) will be revised to become the Diploma in English Language Teaching to Adults (DELTA) after September 1997. Diploma level qualifications are essential for those wishing to move into English language teaching as a career either in the UK or abroad.

Teaching English to Young Learners

Those wishing to teach children rather than adults may take certificates offered by both Trinity College and RSA Cambridge. The well-established Trinity College Certificate in the Teaching of English to Young Learners (TEYL) prepares you to teach English as a foreign or second language to pupils around 6–12 years both overseas and in the UK. The certificate may be especially useful for those with some teaching experience wishing to add a TESOL qualification to their existing professional expertise. RSA Cambridge has recently piloted its new qualification for those wishing to teach young learners rather than adults. The Certificate in English Language Teaching to Young Learners (CELTYL) is designed for those with little or no experience of teaching children who wish to teach the age groups 5–10, 8–13 or 11–16. Courses will last around four weeks full-time. Diplomas in English Language Teaching to Young Learners will be available in due course.

One to One teaching

The ARELS organisation, in conjunction with Trinity College, now offers a Certificate in Teaching One to One. This is designed to enable teachers to understand the principles of one-to-one teaching so they can become confident practitioners able to teach a wide range of individuals from children to business executives both in the UK and overseas. The one-week full-time courses cost around £300. Applicants should already have the TESOL or TEFL certificates and some experience of teaching one to one. Further details are available from ARELS. The address is at the end of this chapter.

Other courses

Some commercial schools such as Multilingua and Berlitz, offer training in their own method with the possibility of subsequent employment within their own schools. Short TESL courses are available via the RSA Certificate in Initial Training in the Teaching of English as a Second Language to Adults. This is designed mainly for volunteers teaching immigrants at home in the UK. It may be useful as a way of gaining teaching experience but does involve a minimum of 100 hours' study time.

QTS courses

A small number of colleges offering PGCEs leading to QTS enable students to take a subsidiary subject in teaching English as a second or foreign language. The content of these courses and the amount of time given to the language teaching element varies. Consult the Graduate Teacher Training Registry *Guide for Applicants* for further details. Contact details at the back of this book.

Other advanced courses

Those wishing to pursue their career further, in managerial
positions, for example, may consider taking courses beyond the
Diploma level. Options include masters and doctoral degrees or a
range of short courses in specialised subject areas. An Advanced
Diploma in Language Teaching Management is being introduced by
RSA Cambridge. Students should study the course content to ensure
it will suit their needs. MA courses, for example, are not designed as
a practical teaching qualification and may be more helpful for those
considering writing text books. The British Council produces a useful
information sheet on advanced and postgraduate courses with
TEFL/TESL content. Contact details for the British Council at the
end of this chapter.

Case Study: Teacher of English as a foreign language

*Anne originally trained to teach languages in secondary schools
but is now working as a Teacher of English as a Second
Language (TESOL) in a London further education college. 'After
I completed a degree in French and German I spent some time
working as an "assistante" in a French university which made it
relatively easy to train to become a secondary teacher of modern
foreign languages. However, I didn't go into schools but ended
up teaching English in Morocco for a total of six years. By the
time I came back to England permanently I had very little
experience of teaching in schools, just one year in a school in
Tottenham, in between two long contracts in Morocco. It seemed
natural for me to pursue my career as a teacher of English. My
experience plus the fact that I had a PGCE and had gained
TEFL Certificate and Diploma qualifications while I was on
my Moroccan contracts helped me obtain a post in a FE college
teaching English to adults.'*

*'I now teach lots of mature students, mainly aged 25 years and
above. Many of these are recent immigrants to the UK and some are
refugees. I also teach English with a vocational emphasis, for
example English for banking or law professionals who need to
improve their English to enhance their job prospects. I find the
students highly motivated and focused. Many of them have been
incredibly enterprising to get to the UK and know that improving
their English could be the key to getting work. Also many of them are
in any case very highly educated but are having to take low-paid
work to help fund their courses. I also teach on income-generating
courses such as teaching French to staff in a large British company.*

'Like any other teacher, I have to keep abreast of my subject. There are new exams that come out and you need to make sure you know what your students will have to learn to pass them successfully. Teaching styles also change and you need to make sure your skills are up-to-date. In my subject the emphasis on grammar is making a comeback but I don't think we will ever go back to how they used to teach Latin. TESOL will always be taught in conjunction with using 'authentic' materials and the 'communicative' style of teaching where we try to use the class to replicate real situations encountered in the outside world.

'I still enjoy teaching and I think a lot of my students are brilliant. There are a lot of pressures on teachers in Further Education, however, and because I have refused to accept a new contract which would mean longer teaching hours and less holidays I haven't had a pay rise for three years. I am thinking of training to become a teacher trainer, helping those who want to become teachers of English as a Foreign Language. Or, I might even brush up my French and apply to become a secondary school teacher, which is what I originally trained for.'

Chapter Thirteen
SOURCES OF INFORMATION

☐ TEACHER TRAINING AGENCY

The Teacher Training Agency (TTA) provides information on the routes and opportunities to train to teach. They provide a Teaching Information Line, open every weekday from 9 am to 5 pm on 01245 454454. Alternatively, write to the TTA, Communications, PO Box 3210, Chelmsford, Essex CM1 3WA. The TTA also has a page on the Internet at http://www.teach.org.uk and can be e.mailed at tta@gtnet.gov.uk

Brochures available include:
Routes Into Teaching
Primary Teaching
Secondary Teaching
These are also available in Welsh. Copies from the TTA or from the Welsh Office (tel: 01222 825 111)
The Licensed Teacher Scheme
The Overseas Trained Teacher Schem

☐ USEFUL ADDRESSES

AGCAS
CSU (Publications) Ltd, Armstrong House, Oxford Road, Manchester M1 7ED (telephone 0161 236 9816).

BEd/BA, BSc with QTS
The Universities and Colleges Admissions Service (UCAS), Fulton House, Jessop Avenue, Cheltenham, Gloucestershire GL50 3SH (telephone 01242 222444).

City & Guilds
1 Giltspur Street London EC1A 9DD (telephone 0171 294 2468).

Department for Education and Employment (DfEE)
Public enquiries: telephone 0171 925 5555 or contact on the Internet at http://www.open.gov.uk/dfee/dfeehome.htm

For teachers trained or recognised in Scotland, Northern Ireland and European Economic Area
DfEE, Mowden Hall, Darlington DL3 9BG (telephone 01325 392123).

For information on work permits
DfEE Overseas Labour Service W5 Moorfoot, Sheffield S1 4PQ (telephone 0114 259 4074).

For the School Teachers' Pay leaflet and other DfEE publications
DfEE Publications Centre, PO Box 6927, London E3 6NZ (telephone 0171 510 0150).

For information on National Vocational Qualifications
National Council for Vocational Qualifications (NCVQ) 222 Euston Road, London NW1 2BZ (telephone 0171 387 9898 / 0171 728 1914).

For information on the Lingua Assistants programme for prospective teachers of languages and other subjects
Central Bureau for Educational Visits and Exchange, 10 Spring Gardens, London SW1A 2BN (telephone 0171 389 4596).

Licensed and Overseas Trained Teacher Schemes
Park Place Training, 1 Princes Road, Ferndown, Dorest BH22 9JG (telephone 01202 897691).

NATFHE
27 Brittania Street, London WC1X 9JP (telephone 0171 837 3636).

National Association of Schoolmasters and Union of Women Teachers (NASUWT)
Hillscourt Education Centre, Rose Hill, Rednal, Birmingham B45 8RS (telephone 0121 453 6150)

NUT
Mabledon Place, London WC1H 9BD (telephone 0171 388 6191).

The Open University PGCE
The Open University, Walton Hall, Milton Keynes MK7 6YZ (telephone 01908 653231 or 01908 652564)
or contact on the Internet at
http://www.open.ac.uk/OU/CourseDetails/pgce.html

PGCE – Guide to applicants and application forms
Graduate Teacher Training Registry, Fulton House, Jessop Avenue, Cheltenham, Gloucestershire GL50 3SH (telephone 01242 225868)

RADAR (The Royal Association for Disability and Rehabilitation) Unit 12, City Forum, 250 City Road, London EC1V 8AF (telephone 0171 250 3222).

RSA
RSA Examination Board, 8 John Adam Street, London WC2N 6EZ (telephone 0171 930 9605). For advice on location of courses.

School Centred Initial Teacher Training (SCITT)
Mike Berrill, Challney Boy's School, Stoneygate Road, Luton, Beds LU4 9TJ (telephone 01582 599921).

Student Loans Company
100 Bothwell Street, Glasgow G2 7GD (Freephone 0800 405010).

The University of the West of England
The University of the West of England, Faculty of Education, Redland Campus, Redland Hill, Bristol BS6 6UZ.

Welsh Office
FHEI Division, Cathays Park, Cardiff CF1 3NQ
(telephone 01222 825831).

Those wishing to teach in Scotland should contact the following:
Postgraduate teaching courses in Scotland have their own clearing system administered by TEACH:
TEACH, the Teacher Education Admissions Clearing House, PO Box 165, Edinburgh EH8 8AT.

For general advice about teaching in Scotland:
Advisory Service on Entry to Teaching, General Teaching Council for Scotland, 5 Royal Terrance, Edinburgh EH7 5AF
(telephone 0131 556 0072)

Those wishing to teach in Northern Ireland should contact:
Department of Education Northern Ireland, Rathgael House, Balloo Road, Bangor, County Down BT19 2PR (telephone 01247 279279)
http://www.deni.gov.uk/

INDEPENDENT EDUCATION
London Montessori Centre, 18 Balderton Street, London W1Y
1TG (telephone 0171 493 0165).

National Independent Schools Information Service (ISIS)
56 Buckingham Gate, London SW1E 6AG (telephone 0171 630 8793).

Steiner Schools Fellowship, Kidbrooke Park, Forest Row, Sussex
RH18 5JB (telephone 01342 822115).

☐ FURTHER INFORMATION

As well as the leaflets published by the Teacher Training Agency you
may find these other publications helpful. Many of them will be
available in career libraries.

Applying For Teacher Training: AGCAS.

Black to the future
A video aimed at increasing the recruitment of ethnic minorities into
teaching. Produced by The University of the West of England (cost
£10 per copy).

Education Year Book, Pearson Professional, 12–14 Slaidburn
Crescent, Southport, PR9 9YF, 01704 26881.
Lists all UK schools, colleges, universities, central and local
government education offices.

Getting a Teaching Job in Further Education 1997, Gay Humphrys,
University of Greenwich.

Handbook on Initial Teacher Training in England and Wales, National
Association of Teachers in Further and Higher Education (NATFHE).
This is a comprehensive list of teacher training courses including PGCE,
BEd, BA, BSc, SCITT courses and the Licensed Teachers' Scheme.

Initial Teacher Training Shortage Subject Bursaries, The University
of Manchester and UMIST Careers Service.

Obtaining Your First Teaching Post, NNT
This booklet gives details of every LEA in England and Wales plus
details of recruiting procedures and advice on completing application
forms and interview technique.

School Teachers' Pay, brochures from the DfEE, the NUT and the NASUWT.

So You Want to Be a Teacher? Guidelines for entry to teacher training for disabled people, RADAR. The Royal Association for Disability and Rehabilitation publishes this guide jointly with Skill, the National Bureau for Students with Disabilities. RADAR also offer advice for those with disabilities who wish to enter teaching.

Student Grants and Loans: a brief guide, DfEE.

Survey of Selection Criteria and Procedures for Primary Courses, AGCAS.

Survey of Selection Criteria and Procedures for Secondary PGCE in English and History 1995, AGCAS.

Survey of Selection Criteria and Procedures for Secondary PGCE in non-National Curriculum Courses, AGCAS.

Teaching: Beyond the Classroom, AGCAS.

Teaching English as a Foreign Language and Teaching Abroad, AGCAS.

Teaching in Independent Schools, National Independent Schools Information Service (ISIS).

Teaching in Schools and Colleges in the UK, AGCAS.

Training to Teach in Further Education, NATFHE.

☐ TEFL

ARELS, 2 Pontypool Place, Valentine Place, London SE1 8QF (tel: 0171 242 3136).

British Council, English Language Information Centre, Medlock Street, Manchester M15 4AA (tel: 0161 957 7755).

National Association for Teaching English and other Community Languages to Adults, NATECLA National Centre,

South Birmingham College, 524 Stratford Road, Birmingham B11 4AJ (telephone 0121 766 6327).

RSA Cambridge, Syndicate Building, 1 Hills Road, Cambridge CB1 2EU (tel: 01223 61111).

Trinity College London, 16 Park Crescent, London W1N 4AH (tel: 0171 323 2328).

☐ USEFUL READING

ELT Guide: The definitive guide to Teaching English as a Foreign Language
EFL Ltd, 5th Floor, Dilke House, 1 Malet Street, London WC1E 7JA (tel: 0171 255 1970).

Teach Abroad, Central Bureau
(tel: 0171 389 4004).

Teaching Abroad
Vacation Work Publications (tel: 01865 241978).

Teaching English as a Foreign Language and Teaching Abroad,
AGCAS
CSU (Publications) Ltd (tel: 0161 236 9816).